Membering the Rhodesian Linguistic Agenda in Zimbabwe

Membering the Rhodesian Linguistic Agenda in Zimbabwe reports on a study carried out in Zimbabwe to ascertain the degree and effect of honouring the colonial linguistic agenda.

The book employs an interpretivist philosophy and qualitative research approach that relies on participatory observations, interviewing purposively sampled informants and focus group discussions involving snowball sampled graduates. It was inspired by the Critical Language Policy Theory that considers language choice a critical determinant factor in how communities are administered politically, economically, socioculturally and educationally. It establishes that whereas linguistic imperialism meant to serve as the lifeblood of the Southern Rhodesian colonial machine, the former coloniser ensured coloniality in Zimbabwe by presenting the English language as a sacred media in political, economic, sociocultural and educational settings forever. The study establishes that the only way Zimbabwe and other such post-colonies could find redemption is by eradicating the sacredness of former colonisers' languages by adding value to all their languages and the indigenous knowledge systems associated with them. It also demonstrates that the bigger the delay, the more is irretrievably lost together with custodians of the languages.

This book will be informative for undergraduates, postgraduates and researchers in linguistics, communication, sociology, anthropology and history. It may also serve well as a resource to government researchers, politicians and other policymakers.

Isaac Mhute is an associate professor in the Department of Language, Literature and Culture Studies at Midlands State University who has vast experience in lecturing, supervising and examining both undergraduates and postgraduates. He graduated with a Doctor of Literature and Philosophy in African Languages, focusing on the morphological, syntactic and semantic representation of grammatical relations from the University of South Africa. His research interests are in both theoretical and applied linguistics (language policy and development, syntax and semantics, onomastics as well as strategic communication issues in education, amongst others). He is a chief examiner for language and literature with an international examining board, professional editor and translator/back translator (English and Shona).

Membering the Rhodesian Linguistic Agenda in Zimbabwe

Isaac Mhute

Taylor & Francis Group

LONDON AND NEW YORK

First published 2024
by Routledge
4 Park Square, Milton Park, Abingdon, Oxon OX14 4RN

and by Routledge
605 Third Avenue, New York, NY 10158

Routledge is an imprint of the Taylor & Francis Group, an informa business

© 2024 Isaac Mhute

The right of Isaac Mhute to be identified as author of this work has been asserted in accordance with sections 77 and 78 of the Copyright, Designs and Patents Act 1988.

All rights reserved. No part of this book may be reprinted or reproduced or utilised in any form or by any electronic, mechanical, or other means, now known or hereafter invented, including photocopying and recording, or in any information storage or retrieval system, without permission in writing from the publishers.

Trademark notice: Product or corporate names may be trademarks or registered trademarks, and are used only for identification and explanation without intent to infringe.

British Library Cataloguing-in-Publication Data
A catalogue record for this book is available from the British Library

Library of Congress Cataloging-in-Publication Data
Names: Mhute, Isaac, author.
Title: Membering the Rhodesian linguistic agenda in Zimbabwe/Isaac Mhute.
Description: New York: Routledge, 2023. | Includes bibliographical references and index.
Identifiers: LCCN 2023019391 (print) | LCCN 2023019392 (ebook) | ISBN 9781032283395 (hardback) | ISBN 9781032283401 (paperback) | ISBN 9781003296362 (ebook)
Subjects: LCSH: Language policy–Zimbabwe. | Imperialism and philology–Zimbabwe. | English language–Political aspects–Zimbabwe. | English language–Social aspects–Zimbabwe.
Classification: LCC P119.32.Z55 M48 2023 (print) | LCC P119.32.Z55 (ebook) | DDC 306.4496891–dc23/eng/20230424
LC record available at https://lccn.loc.gov/2023019391
LC ebook record available at https://lccn.loc.gov/2023019392

ISBN: 978-1-032-28339-5 (hbk)
ISBN: 978-1-032-28340-1 (pbk)
ISBN: 978-1-003-29636-2 (ebk)

DOI: 10.4324/9781003296362

Typeset in Times New Roman
by Deanta Global Publishing Services, Chennai, India

To my late father (Sekuru vaJoe naJay) who always believed in me

Contents

Acknowledgements	ix
Preface	x

1 Introduction   1

   Background 1
   Imperialism versus Colonialism 5
   Informal versus Formal Imperialism 5
   Statement of Aims 6
   Theoretical Framework 7
   Research Methodology 8
   Research Philosophy and Approach 8
   Research Design 9
   Population, Sampling and Instrumentation 9
   Data Recording and Analysis 12
   Conclusion 12

2 Situating Linguistic Imperialism in the Colonial Machine   13
   Introduction 13
   A Note on Key Terms 13
   Place of Linguistic Imperialism in Other Forms 16
   Conclusion 24

3 Political Effects of Linguistic Imperialism in Southern Rhodesia and Zimbabwe   25
   Introduction 25
   Establishment of Colonial Political Control 25
   Impact of Linguistic Imperialism on Southern Rhodesian
      Politics 27
   The Zimbabwean Political Situation 32

viii *Contents*

    Impact of Linguistic Imperialism in Zimbabwean Politics 33
    Conclusion 37

4   Economic Effects of Linguistic Imperialism on Southern Rhodesia and Zimbabwe   39
    Introduction 39
    Brief Background to Southern Rhodesian Economic Base 39
    Effects of Linguistic Imperialism on Southern Rhodesian Economy 41
    Some Highlights of the Zimbabwean Economic Situation 43
    Impact of Linguistic Imperialism on Zimbabwean Economy 44
    Conclusion 49

5   Sociocultural Impact of the Rhodesian and Zimbabwean Language Policies   50
    Introduction 50
    Defining Culture 50
    Sociocultural Effects of Southern Rhodesian Language Choices 51
    Linguistic Imperialism's Impact on Zimbabwean Sociocultural Aspects 54
    Conclusion 65

6   Educational Effects of Rhodesian and Zimbabwean Language Policies   67
    Introduction 67
    Defining Education 67
    Educational Language Policy of Southern Rhodesia 68
    Zimbabwean Educational Language Policy 72
    Conclusion 80

7   Conclusion and Way Forward   82
    Introduction 82
    Conclusion 82
    Possible Way Forward 86

    References   89
    Index   97

Acknowledgements

Firstly, I thank my beloved family for always being there for me throughout this and all other projects despite the considerable economic hardships we are experiencing.

Secondly, my gratitude goes to the editing staff at Routledge for their support throughout the process of producing this book.

Finally, I thank the Almighty for his unwavering support throughout my entire life.

Preface

Every developing nation endeavours to progress towards becoming developed. The journey requires an ability to overcome a variety of challenges resulting from both natural and artificial forces whose effects might be short-term or long-term. However, the fate of post-colonies in this undertaking seems a bit complicated as they must fight both internal and external forces. Their most challenging external forces come in the form of well-calculated parameters put in place by the former imperial powers that have been disguised as harmless or even some kind of blessing for their nations. These are the most dangerous ones as their negative impact might fail to attract any significant attention resulting in the nation's failure to realise the much-needed breakthrough. In some cases, the nation might only understand the need to confront these parameters when it would be too late to mitigate the damage. In this regard, an effort is hereby made to assess the degree to which Zimbabwe has managed to understand the nature of the coloniser's strategy within the nation judging by the degree to which she is geared towards uprooting all of the coloniser's carefully installed parameters meant to derail her emancipation as well as developmental endeavours. Focus is being placed on linguistic imperialism as a major tool that fuelled all other parts of the colonial machine which was also left in place to ensure coloniality way beyond the attainment of independence. Stern efforts are made to ascertain the adequacy of the effort being directed towards uprooting it together with its effects after the attainment of independence in 1980 to establish whether the goals it is meant to achieve are being reversed, maintained or advanced.

1 Introduction

Background

This book reports on the findings of a study on the impact of linguistic imperialism before and after the attainment of independence in Zimbabwe. The study's basic focus is on how linguistic imperialism sustains coloniality in Zimbabwe. Coloniality is hereby considered to be the long-standing patterns of power that emerged because of colonialism, but that define culture, labour, intersubjectivity relations and knowledge production well beyond the strict limits of colonial administrations. In this regard, the book makes a stern effort to demonstrate the degree to which linguistic imperialism acted as the lifeblood of colonialism and its current role in ensuring the progression of the coloniser's mandate in Zimbabwe, even after four decades of independence. The study is quite pertinent since, in one way or the other, colonialism is the main factor that is determining the direction of life and rate of progress towards development in almost every post-colony to date. This is so because, regardless of the efforts the societies make for the betterment of their own existence, the former imperial powers' colonial activities and their short- and long-term effects continue distracting and disturbing them in one way or the other.

To properly introduce the study, the current chapter initiates the process of situating linguistic imperialism within the wider spectrum of colonialism, a goal that is also the focus of chapter two. Colonialism is hereby defined as that form of imperialism involving the transplantation of some surplus population with its natural habits as well as a way and system of life to forcefully implant it in a distant territory, which is either vacant or thinly populated (Bharadvaja, n.d.). Colonialists justified the goal of their exercise as the transformation of the target countries from medieval states often characterised by darkness and evil practices into enlightened, perfect and modern territories. Unfortunately, in almost every case, this enlightenment, perfectness and modernness of the target territory sufficed when judged using the coloniser's lenses. If analysed from the former colony's perspective, the imperial power proved to be the ultimate beneficiary of the entire exercise. She placed her own wishes ahead of the locals' good. For instance, she systematically positioned herself for effective exploitation of whatever resources it desired which has ultimately

DOI: 10.4324/9781003296362-1

made exploitation one of imperialism's main manifestations. This is properly captured by Ocheni and Nwankwo (2012), who argue that the first objective of colonialism is political domination followed by economic exploitation of the colonised country. To fully succeed, the colonialist carefully approached their goal from various angles, resulting in forms of imperialism such as political, economic, sociocultural, educational and linguistic. These presented imperialism with the capacity to totally transform cultures, economies and entire states (Skutnabb-Kangas & Phillipson, 1994) into forms prescribed by (and mainly beneficial to) the imperial powers.

Each of the forms of imperialism had a well-thought-out agenda focusing on the attainment of specified short- and long-term effects, though all of them had a feeding relationship that skilfully facilitated success for each other in the process. For instance, political imperialism availed the power necessary for control of the target country's economic resources which were the backbone of economic imperialism. On the other hand, political imperialism itself had to be sustained by economic imperialism by availing the resources necessary for administrative operations. Similarly, imposing a language policy facilitating the promotion of the imperial power's native language (linguistic imperialism) automatically determined the sociocultural hierarchy in the country by raising the status of the coloniser. This automatically fuelled sociocultural imperialism as the imperial power's indigenous knowledge system, and its entire tradition (including customs, norms and values) was automatically vitalised in the eyes of the locals, resulting in considerable admiration which in turn fuelled the desire to emulate them at the expense of their own. Thus, the sociocultural practices were indirectly and forcefully transferred to the local populace through language (Phillipson, 1992).

Considering the foregoing complex nature of imperialism, the book argues that it is quite critical for every liberation effort to completely understand the impact of an imperialist exercise including an analysis of all forms of imperialism's various effects within that particular society. In the same vein, the book also stresses that every emancipatory effort must be inspired by the levels of establishment realised by each form of imperialism within the society in question. In this regard, the study established that not all liberation exercises must be similar as each fight should be inspired by the actual situation on the ground. As such, every liberation movement must focus on a complete reversal of each one of the forms of imperialism together with their diverse effects, regardless of size and type. The book, therefore, perceives real emancipation from imperial rule as entailing complete freedom from political, economic, sociocultural, educational and linguistic imperialism. It describes the result of such an exercise as the only kind of independence that properly positions the former colony for experiencing and enjoying the fruits of freedom from colonialism since it totally eradicates all potential obstacles from the country.

Viewed from this perspective, it becomes quite unfortunate that most of the African colonies erroneously considered political imperialism (on its own) synonymous with colonialism/imperialism. As a result, their efforts towards independence solely targeted putting an end to the imperial powers' political grip on their nations which meant no proper importance and focus got accorded to the other forms of imperialism, resulting in their effects being either consciously or unconsciously maintained or even elevated after independence. Such situations have seen the former colonies experiencing and battling the effects of these other forms of imperialism way after declaring themselves independent. Unfortunately, the real fruits of freedom from the colonial rule are not forthcoming in such societies as the actual freedom from the colonial clutch was never fully attained due to lack of sufficient efforts to analyse and fully define it before the struggle for independence commenced. In such countries, Zimbabwe included, the entire populace keeps suffering as the remaining forms of imperialism have been so strategically implemented that the former imperial power's grip is ensured in one way or the other. Consequently, should such former colonies decide to totally rule out the former imperial power from the picture, they would be indirectly compelled to ensure their position is somehow occupied by some other superpower as the parameters alluded to earlier demand some place holder. A good example is that of the Zimbabwean administration that feels the need to associate everything that goes wrong with the former imperial power, Britain, despite having over four decades of independence. For instance, the so-called 'illegal sanctions' are often blamed for all economic challenges with the emergency of opposition parties being considered resulting from her regime change agenda. The nation's ultimate effort to totally eradicate the usual stance of continuously sorting for British involvement in the nation's affairs only seemed fruitful after finding an alternative, that is, in the form of the People's Republic of China. This has bred the popular 'shifting from a look west to a look east policy' mantra in the country. Thus, the attained independence is proving to be inadequate as there must be some superpower to look to in the same way a child looks to some parent or elder sibling for their necessary provisions and security. Even way after the introduction of the look east gesture, reference is still being made to Britain and her Western allies as responsible for the country's economic challenges. For instance, having realised people are no longer taking the illegal sanctions discourse so seriously and also the challenges associated with explaining how exactly they facilitate the prevailing problems, the former vice president, Kembo Mohadi, has taken it further as he lamented the economic depression the country has battled since independence from Britain in 1980. Kuyedzwa (2020) notes that whilst addressing the ruling ZANU PF supporters in Gwanda, southeast of Bulawayo, the then vice president castigated all the challenges as the former colonisers' fault as they did not properly teach the locals how to run the economy. This is clear confirmation of the inability to deal with the challenges being encountered in the running of this critical sector of society over four decades after the attainment of independence. This demonstrates how the effects of the other forms of imperialism have resulted in the people's own elected leaders falling so short of living up to the expectations of their electorates, thereby breeding nostalgia for the colonial era within most of the inhabitants.

Considering the situation in question, this book focuses on extrapolating the current state and effects of the former imperial power's linguistic imperialism in Zimbabwe. According to Philipson (1992), linguistic imperialism is a theoretical construct devised to account for linguistic hierarchisation, to address issues of why some languages come to be used more and others less and the structures and ideologies that facilitate such processes. Linguistic imperialism is a subtype of linguicism, a term that Skutnabb-Kangas (1988) coined to draw parallels between hierarchisation based on 'race' or ethnicity (racism, ethnicism), gender (sexism) and language (linguicism). Just as racism studies were revitalised in the 1970s, linguicism studies attempt to put the sociology of language and education into a form that furthers scrutiny of how language contributes to unequal access to societal power and how linguistic hierarchies operate and are legitimated (Philipson, 1992). In line with this, the human rights law decrees that discrimination based on features like race, gender and language is morally unjustifiable and, therefore, countries have a duty to ensure the full recognition of the rights of speakers of 'smaller' indigenous languages (Skutnabb-Kangas & Philipson, 1994). It is, however, unfortunate that the importance of targeting the effects of linguistic imperialism is usually ignored in most cases. In this regard, Mazrui (1997) even questions why the World Bank does not seem to regard the linguistic Africanisation of the whole of primary education and beyond as an effort worth its consideration in the African continent. For instance, he notes how the Bank's publication on strategies for stabilising and revitalising universities makes absolutely no mention of the place of indigenous languages at the tertiary level of African education.

Whilst the position above is the initial source of inspiration for this study, there is also the view that most of the challenges bedevilling various sectors of most post-colonies could be directly or indirectly traced to the parameters implemented during the colonial era and whose solutions would only be fully achieved through proper mitigatory measures for their effects (Mhute, 2021). This book is an effort towards establishing the degree to which linguistic imperialism has been impacted by the struggle for independence in Zimbabwe. It explores the extent to which the parameters put in place by the settler government during the Southern Rhodesian era for the attainment of its linguistic agenda were targeted by the liberation struggle and reversed in the former colony during the over four decades of independence. Efforts are also made to examine the extent to which the short- and long-term effects of linguistic imperialism targeted by the Southern Rhodesian leadership have been properly mitigated to establish whether their linguistic agenda is being eradicated, maintained or even elevated directly or indirectly in Zimbabwe. Efforts are then made to ascertain the kind of damage and challenges caused to date and implications for the future of the post-colony. The book proposes as well the possible alleviatory measures that could bail out the country and others in similar situations from the troubles.

Imperialism versus Colonialism

It is pertinent for such an introductory chapter to define and clearly demonstrate the relationship between key terms. Imperialism and colonialism are two such central words here whose use often overlap. Imperialism refers to the total control of a territory and its people, thereby generating an empire. An empire refers to a society where universal sovereignty is asserted through force, and the term is derived from the Latin word 'imperium' meaning command and domination (Bennett, 1962). Popular examples of empires include the Roman Empire and the Ottoman Empire. Contrarily, colonialism, as highlighted already, refers to the transplantation of a surplus population with its lifestyle and system of government to another territory, usually vacant or thinly populated. This results in a colony. It is critical to stress here that the rate at which the colonies got distanced from their usual lifestyles differed with some imperial powers like Portugal going as far as attempting to achieve a complete assimilation. A good example is the Mozambican case where efforts were made to generate another Portugal away from home by extinguishing all traces of the Mozambican tradition by declaring the use of all the indigenous languages anywhere in the country at whatever time a crime. This is different from the British approach which saw colonies like Southern Rhodesia making efforts to allow some use of two of the indigenous languages, that is, Shona for Mashonaland part and Ndebele for all of Matabeleland, with further efforts being made to have them taught to some extent in the schools.

It is vital to note as well that both empire and colony were characterised by the imperial power's complete command and domination with the only difference lying in the transplantation of some surplus population in the latter. This justifies the use of terms like political imperialism, economic imperialism, socio-cultural imperialism, educational imperialism and linguistic imperialism within a colony as well. This book also explains why scholars like Bharadvaja (n.d., p.3) characterised the colonisation of Africa as 'the new imperialism of the nineteenth century from its predecessors in terms of its scope, intensity, and long-range consequences.' It is the aspect of intensity as well as the range of consequences that the book sets to analyse within the Zimbabwean nation more than four full decades after the attainment of independence.

Informal versus Formal Imperialism

It is quite critical at this juncture to outline in considerable detail the distinction between these two major forms of imperialism as this ensures an enhanced understanding of imperialism. Firstly, there is informal imperialism which is basically a subtle and less visible way of exercising imperial rule. In this case, the local people were allowed to retain their system of administration and the informal imperialism took the form of carving out zones of sovereignty and privileges such as ports as well as spheres of influence or interest. This also took the form of the golden policy to trade without rule and political responsibility (Woolf, 1997). It would be less visible and entailed just some remote involvement of the imperial power and a considerably limited degree of exploitation. On the other hand, formal imperialism or effective occupation is characterised by a direct rule that sees the imperial power deposing the existing government and replacing it with a totally new one. Under this mechanism, different forms were put in place in Africa and Asia such as Protectorates, Concessions and Colonies. This saw complete transformations of the national administrations which was the exact case with most African colonies. In the then Southern Rhodesia, the kings that ruled before the advent of colonial rule were first set against each other and then overthrown through signing tricky treaties whose stipulations were later defended through warfare, paving the way for a white settler government that administered till it was overthrown by the liberation struggle that put in its place the Zimbabwean government in 1980.

Statement of Aims

The imposition of one country's language on another, along with its cultural, social, economic and political models, is what Phillipson (1992, p. 17) describes as 'a movement from the "core" to the "periphery"'. As such, for Philipson (1992), the world can now be divided into two domains: the 'Centre' (the elite or powerful first world countries who have forcefully and strategically placed themselves in the weaker countries' driving seats) and the 'Periphery' (the developing ones who in one way or the other have been forced to rely on their powerful counterparts for direction at the expense of their resources). After the attainment of so-called independence across the world, language has proved to be one of the basic media through which the elite of the 'Centre' regulates the 'Periphery' and plays a crucial function by providing the link between the dominant and the dominated groups. It is representative of the basis upon which the notion of linguistic imperialism has been built and is still maintained. The position is echoed by Penny (2002) who notes that many critics have argued that language is never a neutral vehicle for communication and contextual factors are inextricably tied to it. As such, language is perceived as playing a fundamental role in the promotion of global inequalities and structures of dependency (Mhute, 2021). In this regard, the book explores the current position of the colonial parameters meant for the achievement of linguistic imperialism in Zimbabwe after over four decades of independence. It also unpacks the effects of those parameters in a bid to ascertain the role that linguistic imperialism is performing in deraili ng progress and development in Zimbabwe and many such developing post-colonies. The effects are assessed from a political, economic, sociocultural and educational perspective. Considering how difficult it is to move away swiftly and totally from some of the adopted languages, the book goes on to conclude by proposing plausible solutions for the situation.

Theoretical Framework

A theoretical framework can be described as a research exercise's basic software. It guides the approach to the problem data collection and analysis procedures within the study. It determines the nature of data to be gathered, who to gather it from, how to gather it and its analysis. The current study was inspired by the Critical Language Policy (CLP) theory as presented by Ricento (2006). CLP is defined as a field within critical applied linguistics whose post-modern approach, according to Pennycook (2006, p. 44), 'focuses on establishing how governance is achieved through language'. In this regard, CLP considers language a critical aspect of governance, a position that supports the understanding that language is far from being just an empty code for human association, but, rather, a force that determines how the entire world is administered. This book considers the Southern Rhodesian language policy a major governance tool that in a way enhanced the attainment of all the colonial goals, be they political, economic, sociocultural or educational. This has sparked the desire to explore the adequacy of the Zimbabwean policies in ensuring governance that reverses or, at least, stalls further attainment of these goals of the colonial era.

The economic approach in CLP makes it possible to help social actors assess the pros and cons of different avenues open to them and make principled and transparent choices. The approach, therefore, sees even decisions in other sectors of society such as the economic choices made by different nations as being informed by the ideology behind the adopted language policies. As stated in the introduction, this confirms the feeding relationship characteristic of the different forms of imperialism. Similarly, Schiffman (2006, p. 112) emphasises the relevance of the CLP's concept of linguistic culture, which is basically understood as the sum totality of ideas, values, beliefs, attitudes, prejudices, myths, religious structures and all the other cultural 'baggage' that speakers bring to their dealings with language and culture. This means, through language policy, the entire way in which a complete society is run gets automatically dictated. The theory, in a way, has a bearing on the determination of the religious, sociocultural, educational, economic and political order of the society. In this vein, the current study argues that linguistic imperialism, using language policy as its sole weapon, is the form of imperialism that was used to glue all the other forms of imperialism together. This makes it very certain that ignoring the emancipation of a country from linguistic imperialism would dictate the actual degree of the post-colony's independence from the political, economic, educational and sociocultural clutches of the former imperial power. In other words, the former imperial power would certainly maintain some indirect influence on the post-colony's political, economic and sociocultural order if the impact of linguistic imperialism is either ignored or not properly mitigated. In this regard, the only way the colonial order could be effectively eradicated is through the reversal of linguistic imperialism in all its various forms and effects. The study explores the extent to which Zimbabwe has managed to get rid of linguistic imperialism together with its effects on all of the society's other sectors.

Research Methodology

This book is informed by research that was conducted in Zimbabwe. As such, for ensuring credibility, it is quite prudent at this juncture to outline in detail the research methodology adopted for this study. A research methodology is the specific set of procedures or techniques adopted for identifying, gathering, processing and analysing information on a given topic (Mhute, Mangeya, & Jakaza, 2022). Therefore, it is basically about what data to collect, who to collect it from, how to collect and how to analyse it (Jansen & Warren, 2020). To do justice to all these aspects, there is need to explain the adopted research philosophy, research approach, research design, sampling procedure, data collection and analysis procedures involved. As such, each of them is presented in considerable detail as it was applied to the current study.

Research Philosophy and Approach

An interpretivist philosophy and qualitative research approach was adopted for this study. Whilst quantitative research relies on the collection and measurement of numerical data to describe, explain, predict or control variables and phenomena of interest (Gay, Mills, & Airasian, 2009), qualitative research, according to Creswell (2014), is an approach for exploring and understanding the meaning that respective individuals or groups ascribe to a social or human problem. This is reiterated by Berg (2001, p. 7) who notes that 'qualitative research properly seeks answers to questions by examining various social settings and the individuals who inhabit these settings'. Whilst one of the underlying tenets of quantitative research is a philosophical belief that our world is relatively stable and uniform, such that we can measure and understand it as well as make broad generalisations about it, the basic qualitative research goal is to gain a better understanding of every situation or event. As such, qualitative researchers are most interested in interpreting how humans arrange themselves and their settings and how they, as inhabitants of these settings, make sense of their surroundings through symbols, rituals, social structures, social roles and so forth. The process of this kind of research involves emerging questions and procedures, data being typically collected in the participant's setting, data analysis inductively building from particulars to general themes and the researcher making interpretations of the meaning of the data. Lindlof and Taylor (2002) argue that actual talk and gestures are some of the raw materials of analysis in qualitative studies. This mandated me as the researcher to act as the primary instrument in collecting and analysing the data.

Research Design

A research design is a blueprint for the collection, measurement and analysis of data. In other words, it is the overall strategy one chooses to use in the integration of the various components of the study in a coherent and logical manner (Creswell, 2014). This study adopted a case study research design. For Cohen, Manion and Morrison (2018) and Adelman et al. (1980), a case study is a specific situation that is frequently designed to illustrate a more general principle. It is in fact 'the study of an instance in action' (Watts & Ebbutt, 1987, p. 72). Thus, the focus is on a chosen part of the entire population that is studied on behalf of the whole. The emerging results would then be generalised over the entire population. It is quite appropriate for qualitative research as it allows a deeper analysis of the given topic which is usually impossible with studying the entire population. Since the study focused on the entire Zimbabwean population's perception of the degree to which the national independence of 1980 has effectively emancipated the nation and how much the postcolonial linguistic order is reversing the Southern Rhodesian linguistic agenda, a case study of citizens of varying professions was considered appropriate for the study. These citizens included postgraduates in different fields of study as well as teachers in various schools.

Population, Sampling and Instrumentation

According to Chiromo (2006), population refers to all the individuals, units, objects or events that will be considered in a research project. In this study, all Zimbabwean citizens constituted the population. Apart from observing the activities taking place in Zimbabwe for the past two decades now, I purposively carried out participatory observation of some postgraduates and teachers talking about and reacting to the challenges being faced in the country at the hands of the adopted linguistic policy. I proceeded to employ snowballing, a non-probability sampling strategy that some may see as similar to convenience sampling. I considered it appropriate as it is the best procedure for locating subjects with certain attributes or characteristics necessary in a study but in different geographical positions. Lee (1993) considers it particularly popular for studying various classes of deviance, sensitive topics or difficult-to-reach populations. I considered the topic under study quite sensitive and one for which the appropriate informants might be difficult to identify as people possessing useful insights into the Southern Rhodesian and Zimbabwean linguistic agendas are scattered across the country. I, therefore, identified several postgraduates whom I believed to have the necessary information, based on my usual interactions with them. I then requested them to join my WhatsApp focus group discussion platform at same time sharing the group link with other prospective informants. I encouraged them to share it with interested Zimbabwean nationals anywhere in the world. In total, about 73 members joined the group and participated in the live discussions that took place over six days.

After joining, I proceeded to share with them the focus of the research being undertaken, how the discussions were to be done as well as the ethical considerations that guided the entire study. The latter involved informing the informants about my request for their consent to participate in the study and their pledge not to address any member by name despite how close they could be. I made it clear that the information to be gathered was to be used solely to write this book and also assured them of my total commitment to ensure confidentiality and anonymity by avoiding the use of names in the write-up. Finally, I informed them of their absolute right to withdraw their voluntary participation by exiting the group at any moment without giving any explanation.

Since the goal of the research was to rely as much as possible on the informants' perception of the situation being studied, the focus group study guide had broad questions so that the participants could construct the meaning of a situation typically forged in discussions or interactions with other persons. This is because, as Creswell (2014) puts it, the more open-ended the questioning, the better the researcher can carefully listen to what people say or do in their life settings. As such, the following questions were presented for discussion:

1. What is your perception of the role of language in ensuring the attainment of the Southern Rhodesian imperialist goals?
2. How did the former coloniser's linguistic imperialism agenda impact other forms of imperialism?
   a. Political
   b. Economic
   c. Sociocultural
   d. Educational
3. What notable consequences of the Southern Rhodesian linguistic imperialism agenda were notable during the:
   a. Southern Rhodesian era
   b. Zimbabwean era
4. How much of the Southern Rhodesian linguistic set-up got stopped, reversed or advanced in Zimbabwe?
5. To what extent are the changes made this far ensuring the stoppage, reversal or advancement of the colonial linguistic agenda?

6. To what extent are the changes ensuring a reversal or stoppage of advancement of the Southern Rhodesian linguistic imperialism achievements?
7. To what extent do you consider the current linguistic set-up capable of ensuring total emancipation of the Zimbabwean community?
8. Which adjustments to the Zimbabwean linguistic set-up do you consider capable of ensuring total reversal of the Southern Rhodesian linguistic agenda?
9. Are there any other comments you would like to make about the role of the current linguistic set-up in ensuring total independence from colonial rule?

As the researcher, I had the opportunity to present the questions and facilitate and moderate the unfolding discussions. This availed opportunities to redirect the discussions and at the same time probe for more information where necessary. As indicated by Berg (2001), meanings and answers that arise during such focus group discussions are socially constructed rather than individually created. They also allow researchers to access the substantive content of verbally expressed views, opinions, experiences and attitudes. In other words, they provide access to both actual and existentially meaningful or relevant interactional experiences. This means the discussions availed interaction between informants which is an element of profound importance to qualitative investigations. In this case, the interaction all culminated in considerable examples of the effects of the colonial linguistic agenda in both Southern Rhodesia and Zimbabwe up to a period more than four decades after the attainment of independence. It also yielded commendable suggestions on how the pathetic situation could be resolved for the benefit of the entire populace.

Apart from the focus group discussions, selected interviews were conducted with purposively sampled informants. It is critical to highlight that the process of interviewing is one in which researchers continually make choices that are based on the scope of the research, interests and prior theories about which data they intend to extract and explore further with the respondents and the data they do not want to pursue (Jones, 1985, p. 47). However, Jones cautions that in carrying out the interviews, ambiguity should be avoided (1985, p. 47). The problem of ambiguity arises when the researcher allows the respondents to ramble in any direction they choose without giving specific directions as to the purpose of the interview. This problem can be encountered if the respondents have no clear idea of what the researcher's interests and intentions are. Jones argues that researchers are more likely to get useful data if respondents are informed at the outset about the research topic, even in broad terms, and provided with justification for the researcher's interest in the investigation. As such, in each case, the informant had the focus of the study carefully explained and any possible questions answered.

12 Introduction

Data Recording and Analysis

For the participatory observations, I used a tablet for noting down important information whereas the WhatsApp group discussion saw the shared messages, in the form of notes, audios and videos got automatically recorded for access during the analysis exercise. Selected interviews were recorded with permission. On the other hand, as Berg (2001) notes, qualitative data requires being reduced and transformed to make it more readily accessible and understandable and to draw out various themes and patterns. As far as he is concerned, data reduction acknowledges the voluminous nature of qualitative data in the raw and it directs attention to the need for focusing, simplifying and transforming the raw data into a more manageable form. For the current study, efforts focused on grouping the voluminous data into sections that were then covered under the various chapters that present the basic content of the book. Analysis was essentially thematic to allow a flexible coverage of the matters that emerged during the discussions.

Conclusion

The current chapter has introduced the focus of the entire book. It stresses from the outset that the book is a report on a study carried out to ascertain the degree to which political emancipation without linguistic imperialism falls short as far as the expectations of the Zimbabwean people and other post-colonies are concerned. It specifies that this interest was sparked by the Critical Language Policy (CLP) theory which presents language as a major force in national governance. In this regard, the chapter demonstrates how the book considers a total stoppage and reversal of the Southern Rhodesian linguistic agenda and its consequences quite critical for the effective emancipation of every sector of the Zimbabwean nation. The chapter also outlines the methodology employed in the gathering and analysis of the data whose results are presented in the upcoming chapters. The proceeding chapter further situates linguistic imperialism in the colonial machine by focusing on the power of linguistic imperialism during the colonial era.

2 Situating Linguistic Imperialism in the Colonial Machine

Introduction

Now that the preceding chapter has introduced the focus of the book, and provided some background to the key terms, the theoretical underpinnings as well as the research methodology adopted, this chapter discusses the general role of linguistic imperialism within the colonial machine by demonstrating how it directly or indirectly enhanced the success of the entire colonial agenda. In this regard, a considerable effort is made to show the various ways through which linguistic imperialism impacted the locals and at the same time facilitated the success of the other forms of imperialism in and outside the African continent. This is achieved by uncovering how much linguistic imperialism promoted the total placement of colonies in imperial powers' clutches by justifying the presence and control of imperial powers in the eyes of the locals even way after the attainment of independence. In the process, the chapter proves that linguistic imperialism is a force that many often underrate but whose effects significantly changed the destiny of colonies and post-colonies forever. This is done in a way that confirms Philipson's (1992) argument that the spread of English across the world, for instance, should be viewed as an international activity with political, economic, sociocultural and educational implications.

A Note on Key Terms

To begin with, it is important to define some of the key terms in this chapter, namely, language planning, language policy, language ideology and linguistic imperialism.

Language Planning

In sociolinguistics, language planning, also known as language engineering or language management (Spolsky, 2009), is a deliberate effort to influence the function, structure or acquisition of languages or language varieties within a speech community that is characterised by a multiplicity of languages or language varieties. In most cases, it focuses on determining the languages to be used in different environments by various people of a given linguistic community. Cooper (1989), focusing more on corpus planning or the subsequent development of a language for it to properly perform its given role in society, defines language planning as the activity of preparing a normative orthography, grammar and dictionary for the guidance of speakers and writers in a non-homogeneous speech community. Along these lines, Chivhanga and Chimhenga (2013) perceive language planning as a term that is used to refer to both the process and study of language activities. Chimhundu (1993) also defines language planning as a government-authorised long-term sustained conscious effort to alter a language itself or to change a language's function in a society for the purpose of solving communication problems. Considering his definition, it is pertinent to stress the fact that language is a sensitive resource which makes it critical for language planning to be always guided by the lawmakers of the land's chosen language ideology and it culminates in the generation of the community's language policy. Failure to do so properly might spark civil wars as once experienced between the Tamil and Sinhalese speakers in Sri Lanka.

Language Policy

A language policy is fundamentally the outcome of a language planning exercise that is made part of the law through inclusion into the community's constitution. Canhanga and Banda (2017) define the concept of language policy as the official regulation of the type of language to use in a given institution, organisation or nation with a view to guiding speakers in their social proceedings. At times this might go beyond the social proceedings to include academic and professional interaction of the specified linguistic community. The position is supported by Henriksen (2010) who regards language policy as a set of decisions regarding the languages to be used, their status as well as the context in which they are to be taught. It is, therefore, the subsequent hierarchical arrangement by the function of the languages or language varieties in a speech community. Similarly, Kaplan and Baldauf (1997) refer to a language policy as a body of ideas, laws, rules, regulations and practices intended to achieve a planned change in a society or group's use of language. This is supported by Mhute and Musingafi (2014) who consider language policy as the actions that a government or institution take to determine how languages are used within a speech community, such as a company, country or region. Governmental language policies often reflect the tension between two contrasting types of language ideologies: ideologies that conceive of language as a resource, problem or right and ideologies that conceive of language as a pluralistic phenomenon (Hult & Pietikäinen, 2014). The linguistic policies that emerge in such instances often reflect a compromise between both types of ideologies which makes it appropriate to define and shed some light on language ideology as well.

Language Ideology

Language ideology (also referred to as language attitude or language ideology) is a concept used primarily within the fields of anthropology (especially linguistic anthropology), sociolinguistics and cross-cultural studies to characterise any set of beliefs or feelings about languages as used in their social worlds. Language ideologies expose how the speakers' linguistic beliefs are linked to the broader social and cultural systems to which they belong, illustrating how the systems beget such beliefs. By doing so, language ideologies link implicit and explicit assumptions about a language or languages in general to their social experience as well as their political and economic interests. Thus, language ideologies are conceptualisations about languages, speakers and discursive practices. Like other kinds of ideologies, language ideologies are influenced by political and moral interests, and they are shaped in a cultural setting. Four overarching language ideologies are proposed to explain motivations and decisions, which are as follows:

- Internationalisation: the adoption of a non-indigenous language as a means of wider communication, as an official language or in a particular domain, such as the use of English in the then Southern Rhodesia, India, Singapore, the Philippines, Papua New Guinea and South Africa.
- Linguistic assimilation: the belief that every member of a society, irrespective of their native language, should learn and exclusively use the dominant language of the society in which they live. An example is the English-only movement of some residents of the United States as well as Portugal's colonial language policy in her colonies such as Mozambique.
- Linguistic pluralism: the recognition and support for the use of many languages within one society. Examples include the coexistence of French, German, Italian and Romansh in Switzerland; and the shared official status of English, Malay, Tamil and Mandarin Chinese in Singapore. The coexistence of many languages may not necessarily arise from a conscious language ideology but rather from the relative efficiency of communicating in a shared language.
- Vernacularisation: the restoration and development of an indigenous language, along with its adoption by the state as an official language. Examples include Hebrew in the state of Israel and Quechua in Peru.

Linguistic Imperialism

Although I have already alluded to it in the previous chapter, it is critical to further emphasise that linguistic imperialism fundamentally refers to the imposition of the coloniser's language policy to displace the local languages. It is a term coined by Robert Phillipson and is the title of his influential book published in 1992. Writing about the spread of English across the world, Phillipson (1992) defines English linguistic imperialism as the dominance asserted and retained by the establishment and continuous reconstitution of structural and cultural inequalities between English and other languages. To effectively clarify its nature and impact on a society, he regards English linguistic imperialism as an aspect of cultural imperialism that has its roots in the expansionist politics and ethnocentric ideology of the British Empire. He further suggests that English linguistic imperialism has persisted because of the political, military, economic and cultural hegemony achieved by the United States in the 20th century.

Though resulting in the marginalisation of local languages, it is important, as correctly noted by Gudhlanga (2005), to stress the fact that various colonial powers preferred different language policies in line with their linguistic ideologies. The Belgians and the British preferred a policy of separate development that saw local languages being used and even studied though to a very limited extent. Contrarily, the Portuguese opted for the policy of assimilation in which Portuguese was meant to be the sole language and proscribed the use and teaching of local languages throughout their territories. The Germans opted for a similar policy except for East Africa where Swahili had already gained ground (Wolfgang, 1973).

Place of Linguistic Imperialism in Other Forms

The logical springboard for a discussion on the position of linguistic imperialism within the entire colonial machine is an outline of its role in the enhancement of the other forms of imperialism. As alluded to in the introductory chapter, the imperialists were quite strategic when it came to ensuring the achievement of their goals. They approached their target from various angles resulting in diverse forms of imperialism. In essence, there are four forms of imperialism, though some scholars split them into five or even six. It is critical to emphasise that all these forms of imperialism accorded the imperial powers' total control over the locals and all their resources. They had a clear understanding of how the failure to ascertain their firm control in any one of the sectors would cripple their entire machine. For instance, allowing the locals control of their economy would only serve to cripple the colonialist's political operations. This is the reason Ocheni and Nwankwo (2012) argue that the targeted states or territories were being conquered politically, economically, culturally and socially in addition to being enslaved. In support of the same view, Phillipson (1992) posits that there are, in fact, six mutually interlocking types of imperialism that were imposed by the imperialists, namely political, economic, military, social, cultural and communicative (linguistic). Drawing examples from the African continent and beyond, the various forms are outlined in considerable detail in the following sections with the role of linguistic imperialism stressed in each case.

Political Imperialism

This is the first type of imperialism whose sole focus was on the imposition of the imperial power's political control over the target community. Its primary motive was to take over the power to make and enforce administrative policies within the target society. Since it was never easy for any society to peacefully cede such critical powers to encroaching foreigners, this type of imperialism relied heavily on the police and military forces. These often fought with the locals, in every case taking advantage of their more advanced weapons, to facilitate the imposition of political control as well as its maintenance.

For examples close to Zimbabwe (which remains the focus of the book), Oliver and Oliver (2017) observed that, in South Africa, the establishment of political control was quite unique as it saw the Cape San society falling to violent subjugation that was genocidal in nature, after which it was placed under the Netherlands' administration from 1652 to 1795 and later from 1803 to 1806. It also saw Great Britain taking over from 1795 to 1803 and 1806 to 1961. Although South Africa became a union with her own white people's government in 1910, she remained a British colony till 1961. In 1948, the National Party won the elections marking the beginning of White Afrikaner rule in the country under the supervision of Britain, and in 1961, South Africa became a republic marking the beginning of Afrikaner supremacy over the black people in the country independent of Britain (Heldring & Robinson, 2012). Thus, apartheid rule continued for three decades only to be displaced in 1994 with the rise of the African National Congress (ANC) candidate, Dr Nelson Mandela's election as the first democratically elected president and his successful administration towards the establishment of a new constitution in 1996.

The fact that colonialism was usually a forceful operation that culminated in warfare in almost every instance, making the military and police forces highly significant resources, is beyond dispute. However, it is critical to note that humans are different from all other animals, especially due to their possession of language. They consider it one of their main resources which in almost every case is relied upon before force is resorted to. As such, efforts were always made to establish a common language through which communication could take place between the coloniser and the target society. This is the reason, after establishing political control, the colonisers had to decide on a language policy (in line with their ideology) that would promote communication across the new territory. In South Africa, Dutch Afrikaans, for instance, which emerged as a pidgin language from contact with the Dutch from 1652, proved quite handy in paving the way for political control. Immediately after establishing themselves, the Dutch and the British proceeded to promote the official use of their preferred languages. This saw the promotion of Dutch Afrikaans only to be displaced by English when the British took over control. Due to isolation from the Netherlands, as imposed by Great Britain and inputs from English, French, Portuguese and Malay, the Dutch of the 17th century gradually developed into Afrikaans between 1800 and 1850 (Bostock, 2018). It slowly gained official recognition and its use and that of English (the British's preference) was the background area of conflict for the friction that resulted in two Anglo-Boer Wars of 1880–1881 and 1899–1902, respectively (Giliomee, 1977). All this demonstrates how critical it was for every coloniser to ensure the use of a language policy that upholds their own ideologies. They both tried as much as possible to uphold the use of their languages; even to this date, the two languages have remained quite prominent in that country. The seriousness of the colonisers' dedication to influence the use of their particular languages could be witnessed in 1976 when the decision to impose Afrikaans as the language of instruction over English in black schools resulted in twenty thousand black students getting into the streets to protest. Unfortunately, they were met with police brutality which culminated in the massacre that saw about 180 blacks being killed and more than 1000 wounded. It also saw a state of emergency being declared in South Africa and the detention of more than 11,000 people (Heldring & Robinson, 2012).

Similarly, the voyage of Vasco da Gama around the Cape of Good Hope into the Indian Ocean in 1948 marked Portuguese entry into trade, politics and society in the Indian Ocean world. The Portuguese periodically raided the Gaza state before gaining total control of the port city of Sofala in the 16th century. In the 1890s, a coalition of Portuguese troops and African armies marched against the Gaza state. The defeat of the Gaza leadership in 1897 saw southern Mozambique passing into Portuguese control. In two decades, the Portuguese managed to extend their political control throughout Mozambique. This persisted until a liberation war in 1964 resulted in the attainment of political independence in Mozambique. The Mozambican case was quite special due to efforts by the coloniser to ensure total control over the locals. To this effect, efforts were made to develop another Portugal away from home as alluded to earlier. Language is one major tool by which this effort was to be ensured through implementing a language policy that made Portuguese the sole language for the entire country. They declared the use of any other language anywhere and at any time in the country a crime. Thus, efforts were being made to ensure the coloniser's supremacy by ensuring the extinction of all languages as opposed to their ideological standing. A single neutral language was also meant to ensure unity and peace across the country which made it more governable. Portuguese supremacy was also ensured through the promotion of their native language. It is clear that these types of language policies are political in nature and serve to maintain the existing socio-economic status quo (Pennycook, 2001, p. 50). The same position is assumed by Lin (1997) and Zhou (2000) who suggest that language policies are not independent of political agendas as education and language policies correspond with political agendas and seek to foster similar political ideology in minority communities through a specific education curriculum and language of instruction.

Economic Imperialism

This is the second form of imperialism which involves taking over control of the key aspects of the local community's economy by the imperial power.

It entailed controlling both the production and consumption of the land's resources by the coloniser to facilitate the exploitation of the resources for the benefit of the imperial power. In South Africa, the focus of the Dutch was on amassing as much wealth as possible for their country. They discovered the Cape Colony, for instance, as an appropriate resting point for themselves after very long travels in ships during their trading activities with India (Oliver & Oliver, 2017). As such, the discovery of local forms of wealth such as minerals of different types inspired the desire to achieve the political control alluded to earlier for ensuring total access to it. This saw the Bushman in the Cape Colony, for instance, being annihilated during the 18th and 19th centuries through land confiscation, massacre, forced labour and cultural suppression that accompanied colonial rule (Adhikari, 2010). All this ensured the exploitation of the local wealth. It is also important to note the critical role of the coloniser's language during the exploitation. It ensured coordination of the foreigners' efforts within the society and at the same time placed them at an advantage by participating in a foreign economic environment using their native language. This gave them a big economic advantage in spite of their being foreigners. It is the reason the British Council states that the expansion of English across the world is to further British interests, which are consistently described in economic terms (Goodman & Graddol, 1996). This is why Phillipson (1992) argues that the major objective behind the promotion of English education is economic reproduction.

In the same vein, the Portuguese's interest in Mozambique was on ivory, gold, slaves, rubber and oilseeds, among others, whose abundance they discovered as they were in transit to India for trade. After attaining political control, Portuguese settlers followed in the 1950s and 1960s to take advantage of employment and business opportunities denied to Africans. This demonstrates how much they focused on exploiting the resources of the locals, and it provides a basis to argue that economic imperialism was the reason behind political imperialism. Better treatment was ensured for those locals who quickly assimilated into the target Portuguese lifestyle and one way of judging one's progress in this right was through their fluency in the Portuguese language. Whilst the promotion of only one common foreign language (Portuguese) ensured efforts by the entire society to attain fluency in it, it made participation in matters of economic development easier across the country, though an advantage remained with the Portuguese natives. In spite of being foreigners, it enabled them to delve into any economic endeavour across the country with an upper hand as native speakers of the language of the land. As alluded to already, the linguistic arrangement ensured peace and unity within the country as foreign languages are usually cherished by Africans for destroying ethnicity and the reason most post-colonies can hardly let go of the colonial legacies. The peace and unity ensured productivity, and the consumer of the produce was the imperial power. Having one developed language eliminated the costs associated with developing many languages, thus keeping the money in the coffers of the Portuguese government.

Sociocultural Imperialism

Sociocultural imperialism involved the imposition of the imperial power's sociocultural ways in the entire country at the expense of the locals' tradition. It focused on ensuring that the imperial power's norms, values, religions as well as its typical ways of taming the environment for human survival are imposed on the locals in one way or the other. In a way, this entailed stern measures to ensure a total replacement of the locals' sociocultural practices with those of the coloniser, and one main way of ensuring it was through the suppression of indigenous languages and promotion of the coloniser's language. The role of sociocultural imperialism in boosting economic imperialism may not be overestimated. For instance, it totally transformed the lifestyles, attitudes and preferences of the locals towards those of the coloniser. This brought about the need for the locals to work, earn and sustain their new lifestyle. Indirectly, this ensured cheap labour for the coloniser whose motive was basically to exploit the local resources. It is through this kind of feeding relationship that mining, farming and all other industries thrived in South Africa, Mozambique and all other African countries.

The role linguistic imperialism played in this entire matrix is overwhelming. It is often considered a part of sociocultural imperialism as it reflects dominant attitudes, values and hegemonic beliefs that are to be valued within the new society. It was often castigated for destroying local sociocultural practices at the expense of the colonisers in the same way it promotes linguicism which in turn may be overt or covert, conscious or unconscious. This is so because, just like every other society's culture is always transmitted through language, the colonisers relied upon language to displace local sociocultural practices and spread their preferred ones. Owing to the marginalisation of the indigenous languages during the colonial era, Magwa (2015) established in Malawi that the majority of the interviewed minority language speakers still perceive their own mother tongues (obviously together with the sociocultural practices associated with them) as totally useless and they are extremely shy to associate themselves with them. This confirms the observation made by Maja (2007) that language is the most powerful tool for destroying a people's identity.

Mozambicans were proscribed from using local languages and at independence Portuguese language was declared the language of unity, instruction and government resulting in most of the local languages lacking writing systems and some have not been studied academically many decades after independence with some being threatened with imminent extinction (Mkuti, 1996). The death of a local language is a major blow as it automatically culminates in the vanishing of the intangible heritage associated with it, the indigenous knowledge systems included. The colonialists were well aware of the link which made them so particular about the language policy for their territories and the reason linguistic imperialism is often regarded as the lifeblood of the entire colonial machine.

Due to an understanding of the impact of linguistic imperialism and in a bid to facilitate the reversal or at least minimise its serious impact on locals' sociocultural lives, anti-imperialist-inspired international efforts are often implemented at various levels. For instance, the United Nations Educational, Scientific and Cultural Organisation (UNESCO) Committee (1953) states that the best medium for teaching a child is the mother tongue through which children understand better and express themselves freely. The mother tongue is held to be most significant for our early emotional and cognitive development. Similarly, in 1997, UNESCO sponsored the Intergovernmental Conference on Language Policies in Africa (ICLPA) whose sole focus was to call on governments to create policies that clearly define roles for indigenous languages and the mechanisms for their development and support as well as setting some timelines and targets to be met (Chimhundu, 2002). In the same vein, the 1992 United Nations (UN) declaration on minority rights is the cornerstone of deminoritisation which declared that minority groups must be entitled to:

- The right to enjoy their own culture;
- The right to profess and practice their own religion; and
- The right to use their own language.

Whilst the examples given earlier show how much most post-colonial countries require a huge push to make a step towards reversing the impact of sociocultural and linguistic imperialism, there are some inspiring successful efforts. Owing to the decision to relegate the former imperial power's language, English, to the status of a mere foreign language and accord the official status to Putonghua or Mandarin Chinese, China has rekindled the love for local sociocultural practices. The respect for the language's intangible heritage has been heightened immensely resulting in considerable efforts to treasure indigenous knowledge systems associated with all the local languages. There are efforts to use modern technologies to develop ideas housed in the various local traditions for the benefit of the country and the entire world. A good example is the medical health sector that has seen China becoming one of the global heavyweights through developing traditional herbs of the various ethnic groups into modern medicines. This has gone a long way in assisting the globe in ensuring a healthy society. Of note are the recent contributions the country offered to the globe in understanding coronavirus, its testing, prevention and vaccination. Ricento (2000) finds the 'control and dissemination of culture worldwide to be a greater threat to independence than was colonialism itself' (p. 17), and this book argues that the main way this is done is through language.

Educational Imperialism

One area that got introduced to African cultures is foreign education. Foreign education has contributed considerably to the developments enjoyed across the globe thus far, especially by developed nations. Although it is very hard to dispute the fact that education has proved to be one of the best developments ushered in by imperialists and missionaries as it has the opportunity of bringing about positive transformation to societies, linguistic imperialism impacts heavily on its progress. As such, using countries in Africa, this section tries to demonstrate how it impacts this sector before delving into its effects on colonial and post-colonial Zimbabwe in chapter six. South Africa's language policy saw English and Afrikaans as the official languages until the democratic government that assumed power in 1994 introduced a new constitution in 1996 that officialised the use of 11 official languages for teaching and learning (Ouane & Glanz, 2011). African languages in South Africa can be categorised into four chief groups: the Nguni cluster (isiZulu, isiXhosa, siSwati and isiNdebele), the Sotho linguistic group (Sepedi, Setswana and Sesotho), the Tsonga language cluster (Ronga and Tshwa) and the Venda group (Kamwangamalu, 2001). Whilst the African languages are used by more than two-thirds of the entire South African populace (Statistics South Africa, 2012), the South African constitution recognises nine indigenous South African languages as official. African languages are used as a home language or first language by South Africa's majority, which translates to 80% of the total South African population (Statistics South Africa, 2012). IsiZulu is the most spoken language and a mother tongue to 22.7% of South Africans, IsiXhosa is second with at least 16% mother tongue speakers, whilst Afrikaans has 13.5%, English stands at 9.6%, Setswana is at 8% and, finally, Sesotho has 7.6% (Statistics South Africa, 2012). However, English and Afrikaans are protected in the South African democratic constitution as official languages. This demonstrates how much linguistic imperialism has permanently affected African countries' perception of local languages as there is no such protection for any of the African languages in the country which, in this case, are native to 80% of the population. Contrarily, in Japan, the reasons the Council Report gave for the promotion of the Japanese language are the number of its speakers (the 10th largest in the world) as well as the desire to counter English imperialism (Hatori, 2005), cultivate the attitude of valuing culture and promote enhanced education that fosters respect for the history and traditions of Japan and for diverse cultures of the world (Bunkachou, 2002). Since the Meiji Restoration, the government has vigorously promoted a discriminatory assimilation policy (Hitachi Systems & Service, 2003), and as a result, indigenous peoples are on the verge of losing their languages, cultures and identities. It was only in 1997 that legislation was enacted to substitute the discriminatory former version of Hokkaido Kyuu-dojin Hogo Hou or Hokkaido Former Savages Protection Law with Ainu Bunka Shinkou Hou or the Ainu Culture Promotion Law (Hatori, 2005). This shows that they were worrying about the danger of Japanese to the well-being of other indigenous languages yet other countries are protecting foreign languages at the expense of indigenous languages.

In 1996, the South African Schools Act was passed, which stipulated that priority is placed on realising learners' right to learn in their home language, especially in Grades 1–3 (South Africa, 1996). However, the Act puts the responsibility on school governing bodies to choose the appropriate language to be used, and no direction is put forward. Furthermore, nothing has been done to date regarding African languages. Strategies for implementing mother tongue education are put in schools with no directives on how this can be realised. Therefore, whilst the mother tongue, including vernacular languages, is already used for teaching and learning in the first three years of education (Grades 1–3), beyond Grade 3, African learners are expected to make a switch from learning through their mother tongue to learning through English, which may be a third, fifth or even sixth language. It is for this reason that the Curriculum and Assessment Policy (CAPS) document uses the word 'additional', even though some consider it problematic.

Evidence from the work of Howie et al. (2017) shows that literacy rates in South Africa are very low in all languages, as research shows that most learners in the country cannot read for meaning by the end of Grade 4 or Grade 5. Freire submits that this type of education, of not learning for gist, is the banking concept, as it is essentially an act that hinders the intellectual growth of learners by turning them into, figuratively speaking, comatose receptors and collectors of information that have no real connection to their lives (cited in Micheletti, 2010). This indicates that quality teaching and learning are conceded in many classes, demonstrating the need for urgent intervention by implementing curriculum decolonisation and entrenching mother tongue education. The work by Professor Neville Alexander under the project called Alternative Education in South Africa (PRAESA) made great strides in the discussion of mother tongue education. He argued that education can only happen effectively in one's mother tongue because it is a language that one understands best (Kaschula & Wolff, 2016). Gumbi and Ndimande-Hlongwa (2015) attest to the fact that there is evidence of the informal implementation of mother tongue education in basic education using code switching from English into isiZulu to help learners perform better. They mention the drawback of such an unofficial teaching style on the assessment of learners, as assessments are conducted only in English. This situation is also rampant in other African indigenous classes.

Policies are there to dismantle linguicide in education, but the implementation process is very slow. Since the Constitution of South Africa of 1996 stipulates that every learner has the right to education, this informs the whole globe that some of the African indigenous learners' rights to education have been violated by the mere fact that their education system is 'reluctant' in implementing mother tongue education. Evaluation of the progress made thus far in embracing local languages in the national curriculum in South Africa indicates that the country has not bothered to adopt policies that encourage the use of African languages in the teaching and learning process. As such, the country tends to confine the importance of local languages to the early years of primary school education, thereby accentuating their remoteness and irrelevance to the bulk of the population. Tanzania is perhaps an exception in Africa, as she is reported to be offering a full diploma programme with an African language as the principal medium of instruction (Chumbow, 2009).

Considering the foregoing, it is appropriate to support Maja's (2007) observation that post-colonial Africa saw African governments maintaining and extending the position of European languages in political, economic, educational and social systems. He further argues that this is an unfortunate position as it is happening, although the world's languages represent an extraordinary wealth of human creativity. This is so because they contain and express the total 'pool of ideas' nurtured over time through heritage, local traditions and customs communicated through local languages. As a result, it places most parts of the continent in a precarious position where development remains a dream. This is in order, as noted by Gudhlanga (2005) as well as Mhute and Musingafi (2015) that the countries that are doing well in as far as development are concerned are using their indigenous languages. They argue that there is some link between developed countries and the nature of language policies in use as they all have respect for indigenous languages. Examples are countries like China, Japan, Germany and Italy where English (the so-called international language) is merely taught as a foreign language or a language for specific purposes giving their indigenous languages the opportunity to offer their societies the much-required support.

Conclusion

Using examples from countries other than Zimbabwe, this chapter has demonstrated how linguistic imperialism acts as the glue that holds together parts of the colonial machine. By proving that no imperial power has ever decided to work with the target population's native language as the main medium of communication, among other aspects, it lays bare the role played by language in facilitating the establishment of and viciously fuelling political, economic and sociocultural imperialism during the colonial period and beyond. This has prepared the ground for assessing the position of linguistic imperialism in ensuring the success or failure of all other forms of imperialism in Zimbabwe during and after the colonial era. As such, the following chapter delves into the role of linguistic imperialism in political developments in Southern Rhodesia and Zimbabwe.

3 Political Effects of Linguistic Imperialism in Southern Rhodesia and Zimbabwe

Introduction

Now that the place of linguistic imperialism within the colonial machine during and after the colonial era has been outlined drawing examples from cases in and outside Africa, this chapter proceeds to examine the impact of the language policies adopted in Southern Rhodesia and Zimbabwe. In line with Pennycook's (2006, p. 44) argument that the Critical Language Policy (CLP) theory (inspiring this entire study) 'focuses on establishing how governance is achieved through language', this is done in a way that establishes whether the influence of the Southern Rhodesian linguistic agenda with regard to the political order it intended to achieve is still being maintained, advanced or eradicated in Zimbabwe all these decades after the attainment of independence. The stance is adopted to evaluate the nation's progress towards the attainment of real political emancipation and the role that linguistic imperialism is playing in hampering or ensuring that at a time most post-colonies defend the use of former imperial powers' languages on account of their ability to ensure unity and peace by avoiding any notable focus on ethnic differences and tensions.

Establishment of Colonial Political Control

Historians have been firmly established in travelogues and missionary reports before 1890, and one recurrent theme was that the Africans in the region between the Limpopo and the Zambezi rivers were 'rootless' immigrants without rightful claims to the land, their social organisation was primitive and characterised by superstition and brutal rituals, they lived in a state of constant discord, looting and massacring each other and that there were essential 'racial' differences between the groups, from aboriginal 'Bushmen' through primitively pastoral and often treacherous 'Shonas' to the more respectably organised, but also martially cruel, 'Matabele' (Ranger, 1985a, 1989a). In the 1880s, Cecil John Rhodes' British South Africa Company (BSAC) started making inroads into the region north of the Limpopo River. Rhodes realised how the area was made up of hostile but independent kingdoms with the Ndebele one being considerably

DOI: 10.4324/9781003296362-3

more powerful. Relying partly on the unavailability of proper understanding due to the unavailability of a common language, through missionaries and other agencies, he tricked Lobengula, king of the Ndebele, into signing the Rudd Concession, amongst other treaties, which granted him extensive mining rights. When other concession seekers learned of the Rudd Concession, they convinced Lobengula that he had been duped, and he proceeded to repudiate the concession. He sent emissaries to England accompanied by two disgruntled concession seekers as translators, that is, Johannes Colenbrander and Edward Maund. However, Colenbrander and Maund were motivated by financial interest, not conviction (unlike the missionaries who accompanied Batswana and Basotho emissaries). As such, Cecil Rhodes bought them off and both abandoned Lobengula to work for the BSAC (Woodberry, 2011). Rhodes also used the concession to attain a Royal Charter from the British government, and in 1890 he unleashed the Pioneer Column to invade Mashonaland, marking the beginning of white settler occupation or colonisation (Official Government of Zimbabwe Web Portal, www.zim.gov.zw).

Realising that he had been tricked by the foreigners, Lobengula rose against the white settlers in 1893 which, together with the Shona and Ndebele uprising of 1896–97, saw the foreigners emerging victorious after ruthlessly squashing the locals with their advanced weapons. It also resulted in the asseveration of a tighter grip on the helm nullifying the sovereignty of the locals together with their multiplicity of traditional leaders to a position of insignificance in their own ancestral country. The black people's traditional leaders were being replaced by BSAC stooges. The British government appointed its own officer called commissioner over the British South Africa Police (BSAP) to guard against any abuse of that force as had occurred leading to the abortive Jameson Raid (*The Patriot* August 31, 2017). The tight grip on the reins remained this way until 1980 when the locals emancipated themselves through a bloody liberation struggle that culminated in the ascension of the Zimbabwe African National Union Patriotic Front (ZANU PF) government to power. It is, however, critical to note that Southern Rhodesia had a Legislative Council from 1899 onwards, a Legislative Assembly with the right to pass laws from 1924 onwards, multiple political parties and many democratic elections, before independence (Woodberry, 2011). This should have greatly enhanced the nation's potential for democracy during and after independence (Acemoglu & Robinson, 2005) though this did not happen.

It is pertinent to make it clear that the territory of 'Southern Rhodesia' was originally referred to as 'South Zambezia', with the name 'Rhodesia', derived from Cecil John Rhodes himself, coming into use in 1895. The designation 'Southern' was also adopted in 1901 and dropped from normal usage in 1964 on the break-up of the Federation of Rhodesia and Nyasaland, and Southern Rhodesia became the name of the country until the creation of Zimbabwe Rhodesia in 1979. Legally, from the British perspective, the name Southern

Rhodesia continued to be used until 18 April 1980, when the name Republic of Zimbabwe was formally proclaimed.

Impact of Linguistic Imperialism on Southern Rhodesian Politics

The aspect of linguistic diversity is quite typical of the entire African continent. As such, in these multilingual societies, language planning becomes a critical exercise. However, when the white settlers got to colonial Zimbabwe, the exercise did not attract any considerable attention as they already had a predetermined policy in place in line with their colonial language ideology. However, as I stressed in the previous chapter (that for humans, language is a very important resource in preparing the ground for all other activities) on setting foot in the land between the Zambezi and Limpopo rivers, the white settlers felt the urge to immediately establish some medium for communication with the local populace. They resorted to a temporal measure of using *chiraparapa* and *chilapalapa,* both of which were, in fact, pidgin languages for ensuring communication with the Mashonaland and Matabeleland sections, respectively. Instead of the logical option of the white settlers trying to learn even one of the local languages for use in the necessary communication exercises, since they were very few compared to the local populace, they decided to make the majority of locals learn the unwanted intruder's native language, English. As already stated in chapter two, this proved how much the white settlers valued the promotion of their mother tongue in their target territories. It is the reason Gudhlanga (2005) argues that the colonial masters were eager to impose their languages on all their subjects as a tool for their own administration and power. Furthermore, Kaarsholm (n.d.) argues that the endeavour of these white settlers, just like any other coloniser, was to symbolise the installation and facilitate the perception of themselves as the perfect rulers. Thus, the imperial power's language was much more than just an ordinary vehicle of communication but a symbol of white settler supremacy. This translates to say, by forcefully ensuring its acceptance as the most important language of the land, they forcefully made the entire society accept them as the most powerful and vital race within the entire society. Furtherance to that, they also imposed their language to facilitate a move of the locals towards the British lifestyle by generating some appreciation together with the language.

Chivhanga and Chimhenga (2013) note that proper language planning in the country only started in the 1920s as an activity consciously tailor-made by missionaries who embarked on translating the Bible into African languages, to 'reach the souls of Africans in the most effective way possible' (Roy-Campbell & Gwete, 1997, p. 22). As such, the Southern Rhodesian government officially handed the task of planning local languages to the missionaries who went on to set up different missions in different areas of Zimbabwe. They devised orthographies for the various dialects of Shona, translated the Bible into these varieties and taught locals how to read and write from various centres across the country for them to read, understand and spread the Bible. In fact, these missionaries played a major role in the construction of what we have come to know as the Shona language. However, according to Chivhanga and Chimhenga (2013), they had a lot of enthusiasm but little or no expertise in linguistic description. This created problems of orthographic differences within the same language, such as differences in choice of letters to mark sound spellings, word divisions and word choices. According to Kahari (1986, p. 86), the other source of the challenges is that the research into the nature and structure of the various dialects was conducted rather haphazardly at denominational levels by different missionaries. This is why, having failed in their own attempt to develop a common system of writing for what was to be later called Shona, representatives of the different missions commissioned the South African linguist, Clement M. Doke, to undertake a national language survey in 1929 and make suggestions about a proper national language policy. In other words, the purpose of this Witwatersrand University linguist's visit was to make a thorough survey of the linguistic situation throughout the country to advise the language planners of the government on a uniform orthography and a possible unification of the varieties, for the standardisation of an official language, especially for that part of the country inhabited by the Shona-speaking people. Kaarsholm (1987) notes that through the effort, the colonial authorities tried at bringing order into the existing chaotic situation by homogenising the confusing varieties of African dialects and bringing together the multitude of social and cultural groupings into two main tribes, that is, Shona and Ndebele. This indicates that some linguistic order was critical for the transformation of the community characterised by many ethnic groups into some governable society.

Clement Doke began his study of the nature of the various Southern Rhodesian languages in 1929 and provided a report in 1931 (Doke, 1931; Magwa, 2003, p. 22). The report only came after touring the entire country and was significant for a number of aspects, chief amongst them are the discovery of the mutual intelligibility between five of the languages that the missionaries had already reduced to writing (namely Zezuru, Karanga, Manyika, Korekore and Ndau) and the resolution to treat them as dialects, the coining of the term 'Shona' as the language to which the five dialects belonged and the partition of the country into the Shona-speaking and Ndebele-speaking sections after realising the relationships between the language spoken in each section. This initiated the treatment of these two as the national languages, with English as the official language and all the other 16 languages as mere minority languages without any notable significance within the country (Hachipola, 1998). The minority languages include Shangani, Venda, Tswana, Tonga, Nambya, Kalanga, Sena, Sotho, Xhosa, Khoisan, Barwe, Nyanja/Chewa, Tonga of Mudzi District, Shangani/Tsonga, Kunda, Hwesa and Barwe. The move officially crowned English the lingua franca and most prestigious language within the country and the reason Chivhanga and Chimhenga (2013) argue that English was given the opportunity to dominate the people's political, economic and social lives. This is in line with Chimhundu's (1993) observation that through the arrangement, the African languages were downgraded and vernacularised in the entire society.

Apart from cementing the prestigious role of English in society, the move had its own critical indirect political effects. Firstly, instead of uniting the locals under a single language, such as Shona, which was spoken by around 75% of the local population (Hachipola, 1998), it successfully divided the country into two by officialising and cementing the pre-colonial hatred that used to fuel fights between the Ndebele- and the Shona-speaking kingdoms. In other words, the move acted like a divide-and-rule tactic for the settler government. Woodberry (2011) confirms the position as he argues that, by 1961, the Southern Rhodesian government eschewed any attempt to modernise rural areas and tried instead to re-establish communal tribal life, which they previously had tried to eradicate. They had come to believe that tribalism was helping in keeping blacks 'in their place' (Ranger, 2001, p. 38). It promoted political imperialism by making the role of the government considerably easier as evidenced by the fact that it took too long for the locals to reassemble and wage the second Chimurenga after the first one had been waged and thwarted in the 19th century. Msindo (2005) also notes the impact of these well-pronounced ethnic divisions that resulted from the move adding that, unfortunately, it did not only divide the country into these two sections, but the recognition of Ndebele as the national language, for instance, angered other ethnic groups like the Kalanga who considered their numbers far much more than the Ndebele speakers and yet were being relegated to minority status. According to one informant, they argue to this date that most of the people being considered Ndebele speakers are not descendants of the original Ndebele people from South Africa but rather speakers of other minoritised languages like Kalanga. Secondly, there emerged considerable friction amongst the Ndebele-speaking group from South Africa itself who were divided on the appropriate variety to become the national language with some advocating for the use of Zulu instead as it is the language from which Ndebele emanated. This demonstrates that whilst the position of the foreigner got heightened, the move sow cracks within the local populace.

In addition to that, demotion of all languages of the Mashonaland area to dialects and bunching them under Shona, a newly created language whose name was derived from a derogatory term used by the Ndebeles to refer to them (*etshonalanga*), was a bit weird for their speakers. This was mainly so because the missionaries had already covered considerable ground by promoting the five varieties into independent languages for reading and teaching the bible. Furthermore, the move was more painful for the Kalanga, Manyika and Ndau that appeared ignored completely as only Zezuru and Karanga seemed to contribute considerably to the ultimate standard Shona. Kalanga, Manyika and Ndau hardly had their significant properties, like vocabulary, incorporated and this appeared like a real elimination exercise as language constitutes a people's identity. One good example is the Ndau speakers who, mainly for this reason, kept lobbying for their removal from the Shona language, a goal they only achieved in 2013. Lastly, the relegation of all the other languages to minority status did not go well with speakers of the concerned languages. One informant explained how bitter some of the minority language speakers often become when their languages are identified as such. She indicated how quick most of them would pose the question 'what part of me do you consider minority?'. This confirms the idea of a language as far from being an empty code of communication but rather a significant form of identity demotion and ignoring of which is tantamount to ignoring and betrayal of its speakers. All these scenarios demonstrate the amount of friction that the 1931 linguistic arrangement generated within the entire local populace, thereby indirectly supporting the Southern Rhodesian divide and rule political agenda.

The success of the Rhodesian political project of dividing and segregating is debatable, but there can be no doubt that, at independence in 1980, there was a much stronger tendency for people to see themselves as either Shona or Ndebele than there had been some years earlier. This was also quite evident in the number of obstacles it created for the liberation movement by avoiding total unity by dividing the country into the Shona-speaking and Ndebele-speaking ones. For instance, when they ultimately managed to unite for the common cause, they could only rise as members of either the Zimbabwe African People's Union Patriotic Front (ZAPU PF) or ZANU PF and fought as either Zimbabwe People's Revolutionary Army (ZIPRA) forces or Zimbabwe African Liberation Army (ZANLA) forces.

Demotion of local languages was also meant to make a blow to the religious beliefs of the local communities. As Beach (1994) explains, the languages and the cultures' strengths were readily visible, and they were the ones behind the Shona and Ndebele uprising of 1896–97. The assistance rendered, for instance, by spirit mediums, like Sekuru Kaguvi, Mbuya Nehanda, Mkwati and Umlugulu in these struggles (Moyana & Sibanda, 1984), is well documented as a considerable threat to the establishment of colonial rule. A focus group discussant alluded to popular statements the spirit mediums made like Mbuya Nehanda's *'Mapfupa angu achamuka'* (my bones will rise) which were considered prophesies or inspirations meant to keep the fire of hatred for the coloniser burning as well as the desire to rise in arms again in future alive which culminated in the Second Chimurenga. An understanding of this impact led to more efforts to make the supremacy of English and its speakers more visible to dissuade locals from having faith in anything local, including the spirit mediums who were constantly castigated by Christianity as evil spirits who had virtually nothing to offer other than just drowning people in darkness and all sorts of troubles. The role played by the spirit mediums in the run-up to independence clarifies why such efforts were being made by the colonialists.

As indicated already, evidence of the effectiveness of the linguistically inspired divide-and-rule tactic could be witnessed in the amount of time it took the locals to properly organise themselves against the colonialists. When they finally did so, they could only fight under ZANLA and ZPRA with some activities targeted at eliminating influential members of either side being noticed, demonstrating that instead of the differences between the locals dying down with the colonialist's joining of the kingdoms into a single nation, through language arrangements, they became as pronounced as they were during the pre-colonial times. Similarly, even an end to colonialism failed to totally bring the groups together resulting in the Gukurahundi 'moment of madness' as the then President Robert Gabriel Mugabe preferred to term it. This is when from 1982 onwards the disagreement assumed the character of something close to a civil war that saw a violent military suppression of 'dissidents' and their possible supporters amongst the peasantry in Matabeleland, a situation which continued with varying intensity until the Unity agreement between the two parties in 1987–88 (Anderson, 1983). These events led to a significant strengthening of 'regionalism' within Zimbabwean politics. ZANU PF cultivated its hinterland in the north-eastern districts, whilst PF ZAPU increasingly identified itself with the interests of Matabeleland and came to dominate the political scene in this part of the country.

The placement of English at the heart of all administrative systems, including the judiciary, meant pressure on every local person to learn the exotic language as quickly as they could. The blind eye towards the indigenous languages, which the missionaries had considerably recognised, was quite frustrating to the local people as throwing away a people's language is throwing away its native speakers' culture and tradition as well. It emptied the languages and their cultures' value in the eyes of both white settlers and the locals. It made the locals perceive themselves as incomplete until they develop some fluency in the only significant language of the land and a considerable understanding of the lifestyle that went with it. All this sense of emptiness generated some self-hate that in turn bred considerable appreciation for whiteness and everything associated with it. It acted as a small fire that kept them burning from the inside and was the reason those who achieved considerable progress in learning the exotic language were unable to resist the urge to completely associate themselves with the white settlers. As a result, such people were seriously tempted to abandon their homes and their relatives in favour of the city. In that vein, many marriages collapsed giving rise to new ones, especially in the cities and mining areas. This is the reason the colonial era saw a lot of poems, novels, dramas and songs being composed to lament the city as a threat to the family institution. Harare, a poem in the anthology *Gwenyambira* compiled by Rhodesia Literature Bureau (1979), is such an example of a poem that presented the city as a destructive monster and so is *Tsano* by T.K. Tsodzo (1982), a drama focusing on presenting the truthful nature of the city as a threat to safety and relationships.

As far as progression is concerned, the language policy adopted in Southern Rhodesia facilitated considerable development as the administrators' language was in use. This was a proper platform for progress as it ensured extraction and implementation of political ideas from the English tradition. In other words, by using English, they facilitated the generation of another England away from Europe where English policies could be readily implemented which made development along the English ways more of a certainty. It facilitated a continuation of the English political agenda in the then Southern Rhodesia. Thus (adapting Mhute (2014)), an English language for an English system of administration by native English speakers was the most appropriate recipe for development. The focus group discussants observed how even to date, elderly people are often heard in anecdotal communications applauding Ian Smith's rule in Southern Rhodesia. The participants have even pointed at this as the reason for the comparisons that are often made between Southern Rhodesia and Zimbabwe under both the late former president Robert Gabriel Mugabe and President Emerson Dambudzo Mnangagwa. The language factor, therefore, explains why the colonial administration is often considered much better compared to the post-colonial one, not only for the white settlers but for the oppressed local blacks as well.

The promotion of English and its success that resulted, according to Moyo (2002, p. 152), in its association, together with its native speakers, with diverse kinds of power such as the power to rule like the white men did, power to influence and initiate, power to inspire positive change and power to free oneself from the claws of poverty, oppression, ignorance, homelessness and many more. It became associated with sophistication and all that is first class. Even in anecdotal conversations, people are often heard confessing the respect and admiration they still have for the white man during the colonial time. I heard one elderly person saying

> '*usatamba nemurunguzve iwe, munhu uya akapiwa ungwaru naSamasimba'; nguva yaSmith zvinhu zvanga zvakanaka izvi; mari shoma yataitambira yaitenga zvinobatika*'

(you must not play with the white man, that person was granted wisdom by the Almighty; during Ian Smith's era things were perfect; the little money we got as remuneration bought tangible things). Thus, confidence in everything that is typical of the whites grew so much that, despite all the colonial injustices, the Zimbabwean community is considerably nostalgic for their administration. It is also a clear sign of lack of confidence in the locals' leadership which points to some missing links in the post-colonial administration.

The Zimbabwean Political Situation

Zimbabwe is struggling politically with her more than four decades of political independence being characterised by unprecedented levels of absence of the rule of law, cracking on dissent, a coup, contested leadership legitimacy and disputed elections. A notable highlight is the 2008 election re-run that saw a lot of people losing their lives and others being injured resulting in the withdrawal of the late Movement for Democratic Change leader, Dr Morgan Richard Tsvangirai, who had won the election but with less than the constitutionally required 50% +1 vote. Political challenges continued rocking the country even after ZANU PF reclaimed its superiority through an outright win in the 2013 elections, chief amongst them being the factionalism that resulted in the 2017 coup. The administration could not live up to the entire populace's expectations resulting in a lot of public discontent as raised by the informants of this study. They highlighted instances of people who even get victimised for practising their constitutional rights such as peaceful demonstrations for a review of their working conditions or safeguarding their vote. All this point to a real problem within the Zimbabwean arena, one that the current book sets to account for from an entirely linguistic perspective.

Impact of Linguistic Imperialism in Zimbabwean Politics

It is beyond dispute that linguistically, Zimbabwe has not been considerably emancipated. In principle yes but in practice there is almost nothing done to properly stall the force of linguistic imperialism. This is in line with Chivhanga and Chimhenga (2013) who note that Zimbabwe has inherited British linguistic policies that derive from a colonial policy which, according to Mkanganwi (1992, p. 9), emphasised separate development for the different races, with a political counterpart in the theory and practice of indirect rule. It has dominated as the language of administration, amongst others. Nyaungwa (2013) reiterated the view by asserting that the colonial regimes and their language policies alienated people from their languages and the situation remains the same in independent Zimbabwe. In line with upholding the Southern Rhodesian language policy, the then Zimbabwean President, Robert Gabriel Mugabe, inherited an administrative system designed to serve the interests of the Southern Rhodesian regime as he had the mandate to avoid stalling progress in national development (Mhute, Jakaza, and Mangeya, 2021). This was reiterated by informants for this study who argued that up to this point,

> *'the entire system of administration is modelled along the Southern Rhodesian way and no efforts are likely to be implemented anytime soon to deviate from it'.*

Thus, apart from the withdrawal of the seats that had been designated to the whites, the system has not significantly moved from the inherited one. This means foreign policies and a foreign administrative system are implemented this time using a foreign language by indigenous people. Such a platform is inappropriate for success as far as Mhute and Musingafi's (2015) line of argument is concerned. This is the reason, despite the leadership qualities that the presidents possess, as stressed by the focus group discussion, political problems are being encountered in the country for all these years of political independence.

An amendment of the language policy was only introduced in 1981 through a directive by the Ministry of Education which made English an optional subject for the school-leaving certificate just like Shona and Ndebele and only required one to pass any of the three to proceed to higher education or get a job (Government of Zimbabwe, 1987; Hungwe, 2007). It meant a pass in one of Shona, Ndebele and English would warrant one an opportunity to proceed and, thus, place the three languages at the same level. This was a very significant effort in partially reducing the status of English from its hegemonic position during the Rhodesian era. However, this was short-lived since in 1985, following resistance from white-led colleges, the University of Zimbabwe and businesses, the President could not do anything other than revoke this noble policy. This confirmed the importance of the former coloniser's arrangement of keeping the foreign language at the heart of the nation as well as the voice of the English speakers well after independence. Following the revocation, the government made a new set of provisions for language in education through the Education Act of 1987. As noted by Hungwe (2007), the Act was strikingly consistent with the Phelps-Stokes recommendations of the Rhodesian era which signalled the restoration of the position of English and its speakers' position within the society. This is evident in the provisions which are as follows:

1. The three main languages of Zimbabwe, namely Shona, Ndebele and English shall be taught in all primary schools from the first grade as follows:
   a. Shona and English in all areas where the mother tongue of the majority or the residence is Shona, or
   b. Ndebele and English in all areas where the mother tongue of the majority or the residence is Ndebele.
2. Prior to the fourth grade, either Shona or Ndebele may be used as the medium of instruction depending upon which language is more commonly spoken and better understood by the pupils.
3. From the fourth grade, English shall be the medium of instruction provided that Shona or Ndebele shall be taught as subjects on an equal time allocation as the English language.
4. In areas where minority language exists, the Minister may authorise the teaching of such languages in primary schools (Government of Zimbabwe, 1987).

The revisions to the Education Act of 1987 that were put in place in 1991, 1994, 1998, 2001 and 2004 maintained most of the aspects mentioned earlier with regard to the status of English as the sole official and most important language in the country. Very few additions were made on the way, like the promotion of six minority languages to the status of official minority languages. Shona and Ndebele remained paired as national languages just below the official, English, and the reason Mutasa (2003, p. 304) supports the notion is that 'parents perceive English as the answer to their children's problems in that at present, unquestionably English is the gateway to success socially, politically and economically'. In line with this linguistic configuration, for continuity in politics, the late Robert Gabriel Mugabe also served as prime minister and chose to follow a pragmatic course designed to reassure the remaining whites, whose skills were critical to the country, that there was room for them to continue peacefully staying and contributing to the country. He abided by the constitution's guarantees of substantial parliamentary representation for whites and ensured their representation in the cabinet by handing them two seats. He also formed a coalition government between the two parties and accorded 22 ministry seats to its members with Joshua Nkomo scooping the powerful Home Affairs Ministry. Hence, Noyes (2020) observes that Mugabe's first years in office were hailed up by most international actors as a post-conflict success story and a shining example of racial reconciliation. This also demonstrates the influence of English, Shona and Ndebele in the politics of the land as well. However, it is critical to note that the division created between the locals into Shona and Ndebele was too strong resulting in friction that resulted in the Gukurahundi atrocities alluded to earlier. It has kept on disturbing the relationship between the two sides despite the unity accord being signed between the two leaders of the sides, Robert Mugabe and Joshua Nkomo, merging of ZANU PF and PF ZAPU into ZANU PF, the declaration of 22nd December a holiday to commemorate the agreement and efforts to ensure the second of the two vice presidents is Ndebele. This also fixed the position of the Shona and Ndebele in the politics of the country with the marginalised language speakers rarely surfacing in the higher administrative positions of the country, with the highest they ever got being when a Tonga speaker, Advocate Jacob Mudenda, became a speaker of parliament. This literarily means that due to the language policy–inspired division, talent for the national presidency is only expected to come from the two languages, Shona and Ndebele, with the Ndebele candidate eligible only for the second vice presidency. This is quite unfair to all the other languages and the nation as talent knows no language. This book perceives this as the explanation for the challenges of various magnitudes bedevilling the African country and the reason transformational political ideas capable of making nations graduate from being developing to developed are so long overdue.

Unfortunately, this colonial language policy inspired division imposed in the country is also impacting other political parties that are formed within the country way after colonialism and the Gukurahundi atrocities, even before they get closer to the chance to rule. For instance, I can give an example of how the Movement for Democratic Change that was formed in 1999 and led by the late former Prime Minister, Dr Morgan Tsvangirai, had in place a Shona leader as well as a Ndebele deputy Dr Thokozani Khupe. The Citizens Coalition for Change formed in 2022 is another good example with its leader Nelson Chamisa and deputy Tendai Biti who are Shona and the second deputy, Professor Welshman Ncube, who is Ndebele. This proves that, instead of worrying about issues like gender balance, they are extremely conscious of the representation of Shona and Ndebele within the top administration. Focus group discussants for this study highlighted that a party's failure to do so is considered an obvious ticket to its failure as the Ndebeles would not vote for a party whose leadership does not recognise them. Unfortunately, no one ever bothers to talk of failure to recognise the 16 languages marginalised by the 1931 report crafted by Clement Doke, and no one seems to care about their position within the country's political set-up. It all demonstrates how the political landscape has been given a permanent mark as well by the colonial language policy–inspired division between the locals that was meant to enforce the divide-and-rule ideology of the colonial master.

At least some hope only emerged when the Constitution of Zimbabwe Amendment No.20 Chapter 1 Section 6 (2013) (binding to date) totally reversed everything by officially recognising 16 languages in the country as official. It recommends the official use of all these languages, their use as languages of instruction and their teaching where they are native. This means it makes all 16 languages equal and, thus, removing the roles of Shona and Ndebele as the national languages and English as the sole official language. In other words, it meant English would not be the sole language of administration in the country as its role has become equal to that of the 15 indigenous languages. However, this has just ended up in principle, whilst in practice, nothing changed from what was in place before 2013 (Mhute, Jakaza, & Mangeya, 2021). The position of English is still intact and the enmity originating from the colonial policy is still alive.

To demonstrate the presence of the post-colonial effects of the division of the coloniser's language policy made on the country, one can refer to the friction between the Shona and Ndebele speakers that keeps resurfacing. This has been captured by the ZW News on 17 October 2022 when President Emerson Mnangagwa launched the consultative and engagement process regarding the early 1980's disturbances in the Matabeleland region (Gukurahundi) at the state house with chiefs expected to spearhead the process in the affected communities. This is captured in the image in Figure 3.1.

It is a clear testimony of how the Zimbabwean language policy is struggling to erase the effects of the former imperial power's linguistic imperialistic agenda decades after independence and how much the national administration has remained captured in the issues.

Figure 3.1

Conclusion

After demonstrating how much the linguistically inspired division of the country into two halves, Shona speaking and Ndebele speaking, is influencing the national political decisions, I can assert with confidence that the agenda of the Southern Rhodesian linguistic imperialism is yet to be disturbed by the attainment of independence. Despite a language policy crafted in 2013, which raises the number of official languages whose status is considered to be equal, in practice, no significant changes have been made to the policy of the colonial era. As such, the administrative system in place within the country is still the one inherited from the former imperial power, and the reason former

Southern Rhodesian Prime Minister, Ian Smith, once said he never knew that the locals were only fighting to change the name of the country adding that, had he been aware of it, he would have granted it to them. This is a clear testimony of how nothing was really changed politically. The political landscape seems as well to be permanently placed under the order created by the colonial language policy that promoted a rift between the Shona and Ndebele with others marginalised immensely to minority languages. Instead of gaining, the system is deteriorating as the permanent place created for English is forcing locals to continue implementing policies foreign to them, a move that is bound to fail, hence, the record of poor governance, corruption by top levels and other bad experiences in the country. Considering all this, the chapter concludes that the use of English and the administrative policies associated with it by non-English natives is inappropriate. The next chapter delves into the economic influence of the Southern Rhodesian linguistic arrangements.

4 Economic Effects of Linguistic Imperialism on Southern Rhodesia and Zimbabwe

Introduction

Having stressed the impact that linguistic imperialism has had and is still having on the country's political landscape in the previous chapter, it is proper to dedicate this chapter to evaluating its impact on the economy as well. The rationale for this lies in the fact that in line with the Critical Language Policy (CLP) (Ricento, 2006) theory which inspired the study, language is an entity far from being an empty code for sharing information but rather a resource that dictates how the entire society is administered, even economically. The chapter similarly interrogates the economic implications of the adopted language ideology. This is done in view of the general observation that language is at the heart of every society and the adopted language would never betray its traditional owners' approach to reality. As such, it becomes impossible for it to spearhead proper economic development with foreigners who have no link to its traditional wisdom or knowledge system. This is in line with Mazurui's (1981) observation that no country has ever developed using a foreign language. In this regard, an effort is being made here to assess the language policy adopted by the Southern Rhodesian government and its impact on the economy and how the Zimbabwean one reverses, maintains or even advances the effects of linguistic imperialism on the country's economy.

Brief Background to Southern Rhodesian Economic Base

As captured by *The Patriot* of 31 August 2017, the British South Africa Company (BSAC) administration under Cecil John Rhodes (a diamond mining magnate and South African politician who has always been trying to gain control of mining rights in the interior (Woodberry, 2011) encouraged immigration to Southern Rhodesia by offering European settlers land in the country's climatically best regions. Demand for land by these white colonial settlers, especially agricultural land, increased as investments in the mining sector rose. A good example confirming this is when the government set up the Morris Carter Commission (1925–1926) to make recommendations about what to do with the 45% of the land that was still 'unassigned'. The

DOI: 10.4324/9781003296362-4

Commission recommended segregating blacks and whites and giving virtually all the 'unassigned' land to whites, a move that angered the indigenous people a lot. The mines recruited large numbers of labourers whose demand for food rose yearly. As an incentive, European immigrants were assisted with establishing themselves in farming and mining. In Southern Rhodesia, the average size of a farm was 3000 acres, the same size promised to each Pioneer Column member in 1890 and exactly the same acreage promised to each white person who joined BSAC forces against King Lobengula's warriors in 1893. To get such lands, the BSAC administration grabbed land from the Africans without any qualms, dumping the indigenous people on unhealthy, arid and infertile regions unfit for farming which was the basis of their livelihood. For instance, as early as 1895, the BSAC had identified the Gwaai and the Shanghai native reserves to absorb the Matabeleland landless black people. In 1915, a commission estimated that Southern Rhodesia had 732,153 Africans and that, of these, 405,326 were living on reserves (*The Patriot*, 31 August 2017). This meant robbing them of their priceless ancestral inheritance as well as a destruction of the basis of their survival. That, coupled with the European demand for agricultural land as stated above, created serious inter-racial hostility.

The foregoing demonstrates that the BASC allowed the white colonial settlers to turn as much of the arable land as possible into their own farms and mines without bothering about the impact this would have on the local blacks who rightly owned it. The damage got heightened by the effort to reward the settlers even further, which saw them getting huge stretches of land rich in minerals for mining purposes. The produce from these farms and mines was channelled to the newly constructed industries for processing, and all this was sustained by the cheap labour provided by the locals who were forced to work to raise money for paying the newly imposed taxes like the hut tax as well as paying for the goods that came with the English lifestyle, amongst other expenses. Thus, the settler administration resulted from political imperialism-imposed policies that made it obligatory for the locals to cheaply sell their labour as a way of promoting economic imperialism. The same applies to the lifestyle that came with the promoted English language which boosted the desire for money.

Since it was a promotion of English together with its economic policies by English natives, the national economy flourished considerably during the colonial error. It even saw the country's economy performing extremely well for almost a decade after independence with the Zimbabwean dollar at par with the British pound (thus, better than the US dollar) and the country serving as 'the breadbasket of Southern Africa'. This is a status whose unexpected death and its replacement by the current so-called basket case still shocks almost everyone to this date. This means the country has moved from being the entire region's saviour to its common problem, a disturbing scenario the research tries to account for from a linguistic perspective.

Effects of Linguistic Imperialism on Southern Rhodesian Economy

In Southern Rhodesia, the limited roles accorded to the local languages together with the decision to make official a language spoken by only a minority, English, demonstrated the importance of the imperial power's language to the attainment of the colonial goal. To explain this, Phillipson (1992) notes that language choice in a colonial set-up is ideological, that is, it is totally determined by the colonial administrator's choice of ideology. As such, in Southern Rhodesia it involved the imposition of a language policy of the imperial power's choice which had English as the official and language of instruction. They focused on the generation of beliefs and attitudes that glorify them together with their dominant language, stigmatise others and rationalise the linguistic hierarchy together with exploitation, injustice, inequality and hierarchy that privileges those able to use the dominant language. In short, the focus was just on generating a hegemonic societal dominance of the coloniser through the language. So, the language within the colonial machine was more of a force through which the place of the imperial power was internalised and naturalised as being normal to neutralise the logical urge to oppose and rise against the intruder.

As already indicated in chapter three, the coloniser was so concerned about ensuring that English become the most prestigious language of the land. This forced the settler government to make stern efforts to promote immigration of native English speakers by offering them farm and mining land in the country. This was meant to generate a considerable elite section of the society sustaining a native English culture that would spread to the locals who constituted the majority of the population, since for people to learn a second language effectively they need exposure to the language and its culture. It resulted in a sizeable upper class whose lifestyle every one of the locals was bound to admire and wish to be part of.

The move created a society characterised by classes. A considerable gap between native English speakers and those locals speaking indigenous languages. English speakers became farm and mine owners. They were also promoted into employers who availed jobs to the locals who were now bound to raise funds for various expenses introduced by the new arrangement. In a way, whilst the native English speakers could work but only in managerial and other decision-making positions, the local language speakers were turned into insignificant people whose survival depended on the mercy of the English speakers. They were only considered fit for the provision of cheap unskilled labour as they struggled to understand the issues critical to the workplace due to lack of proficiency in the English language. This made the ability to speak English and sustain a typical English lifestyle a cherished attribute that would warrant better employment opportunities in the country. The focus group discussants also stressed the value of fluency in the English language during the colonial era as it made the master's job much easier. It availed someone who easily and perfectly understood the necessary instructions and, in some cases, provided intermediary services between the master and the local workers. This made fluency in English one of the most important qualifications for being hired and promoted even to this day. Such people were also considered appropriate for supervisory roles which stimulated the condition for job applications and interviews to be done in English. The coloniser subsequently went on to make English the only specified compulsory language subject to be passed together with Mathematics and any other three for a person to be employable, a condition in place to this very day for most posts.

The desire to generate perfect labourers for the farms, mines and industries out of the indigenous language speakers influenced the nature of education given to them as well. English became the language of instruction for all the subjects and efforts were being made to prove the local languages valueless. The history, science, economics and geography syllabi were designed to redefine the locals' perception of the world and expose them to the English lifestyle that was based on money as much as possible. This perception was also appropriate for ensuring all locals develop an admiration for the English lifestyle and also try their level best to assimilate themselves into it.

In line with Mazrui's (1981) assertion, by making English the official language of business in a country where English speakers had been made the most important people politically, economically and socioculturally, the country made an appropriate background for economic development. It meant the country was being run along the traditional ways of the administrators using their native language. As expected, this resulted in considerable economic development in Southern Rhodesia. According to the World Bank (https://documents.worldbank.org), Southern Rhodesia was a member of the Commonwealth, and in 1923, when she secured responsible government, the European population was around 35,000 and the considerable wealth of the country was derived almost wholly from gold mining. Southern Rhodesia was heavily dependent on exports as one-half of the total output was being exported. Tobacco grew to become the most important export, next in importance being gold, asbestos, manufactured goods (clothing, cigarettes and footwear) and chrome. This demonstrates how the English way of life became the basis for the country's economy, allowing continuity of the progress that was being made in England, though with more resources this time. Thus, confirming the assertion that proper development is possible when it is based on the community's traditional way of survival.

The foregoing means the decision to demote all indigenous languages in Southern Rhodesia could not have any notable negative implications on the economy as the colonialists decided to bring a new upper class with its new system of survival. In fact, it brought about the appropriate parameter for success by ushering in a continuation of the English language and economic ways by English people in a place where more land and resources were guaranteed, unlike in England. It ensured that the produce from the new territory easily found itself in international markets like the Commonwealth countries. For instance, this led to the rise of organisations like the Cold Storage Commission (CSC) which became so popular for supplying quality meat but eventually struggled to survive after independence when Zimbabwe got booted out of the Commonwealth, readmission into which is not forthcoming to this date.

The Southern Rhodesian linguistic configuration also meant elimination of expenses associated with the development of local languages. Only Shona and Ndebele were marginally developed basically by the missionaries who intended to promote the spreading of the gospel to all parts of the country. This had economic benefits for the colonial government as language development usually offers more of the long-term benefits which they would not have enjoyed. Thus, to the colonial government, the multiplicity of the local languages was more of a liability than a resource. Savings from language development were boosted by the fact that English had already been developed with teachers and books readily available for importation. Furtherance to that, teachers were easily lured as they were ensured of working within an environment more of a home away from home. This was boosted by the incentives offered by the BSAC to white settlers who were prepared to come to Southern Rhodesia.

Some Highlights of the Zimbabwean Economic Situation

It is fundamental to considerably stress that the Zimbabwean economy is struggling for the greater part of the over four decades of independence. It has broken global records in areas such as hyperinflation, low wages, unemployment rate, high cost of living, corruption, electricity blackouts, poverty (with the majority surviving on less than a dollar per day) and having critical sectors crippled by loss of experienced personnel to brain drain. Despite efforts made to withdraw land and mines from the whites, amongst others, the suffering has remained the order of the day which suggests the presence of some missing link within the country's economic parameters.

For some evidence of the challenges being experienced, as of 12 November 2022, the country's inflation is averaged at 86.11% after reaching an all-time high of 837.53% in July 2020 since the 2009–2013 Government of National Unity with the highest-ever rate being the 79,600,000,000% per month with the year-over-year inflation rate reaching an astounding 89.7 sextillion percent in 2008. On 9 November 2022, *Pindula* news published a story entitled 'Government Invites Retired, Former Nurses and Health Workers Back into Service'. The story explains how the Ministry of Health and Child Care (MoHCC), through the Health Services Board (HSB), has extended the waiver to reappoint former health workers who desire to re-join service, a move that was being made to fill up the gaps that have arisen as a result of the mass exodus of skilled personnel mainly to Western countries due to the unfavourable working conditions and poor remuneration at home. Similarly, the *NewsDay Weekender* of 9 November 2022 published a story entitled 'Staff exodus affects critical mass at state universities'. The story reports Great Zimbabwe State University's loss of 50 academics, five of them PhD holders through resignations in the year 2022 alone. This shows how critical sectors of society are being crippled by brain drain due to the unending economic challenges. The fact that national education has the capacity to produce experts on demand in first world countries demonstrates that their failure to turn around their own economy has some special explanation behind it.

Impact of Linguistic Imperialism on Zimbabwean Economy

As explained in considerable detail in the previous chapter, the English language is still the only de facto official language in Zimbabwe. Although the 2013 national constitution theoretically places it at the same level as 15 other official indigenous languages, in practice, English has retained its usual status as the sole official language. Economically, it has maintained its position of being the only necessary language subject for employment even for cleaners at organisations and interviews are still conducted in it. It is also the language recognised at every white-collar workplace. In other words, it is the language in which meetings and other workplace communications take place, a condition that focus group discussants say has offered no room for contributions of those struggling with the language. The informants further indicated that even in conducting business locally, with only native speakers of the same indigenous language involved, English still maintains its position as the language of business. Business proposals are still assessed in it, and there seems to be no desire to turn back any time soon. The ability to write the proposal perfectly in the English language determines whether one gets a tender or not. This illustrates the special link between linguistic imperialism and economic imperialism which yielded its tag as the lifeblood of the entire imperialist machine.

Unfortunately, key sectors of society flourish when they are run using the popular medium. This is the reason Chivhanga and Chimhenga (2013) argue that extensive economic growth can only be achieved through communication and interaction of different socio-economic factors in a language spoken and understood by the majority. It is in line with Mackey (1979) who notes that when people's inalienable linguistic rights are acknowledged, the full invaluable participation of everyone, including the minority groups, in all pertinent national activities, such as judicial and administrative proceedings, civil service, examinations, voting and public employment, is guaranteed. For instance, using an official language like Shona as a language of official business communication in the Mashonaland area would benefit the country as it is the language spoken by most of the population (currently estimated to be more than 80% of the entire country). It would ensure the active participation of most of the populace since effective communication is considered the major secret behind humans' ability to surpass all other primates and effectively tame the entire world. The position is shared by Mutasa (2004, p. 240) who considers language one of the most precious possessions of mankind, as it is the principal factor that enables individuals to become fully functioning members of the group into which they are born. In this regard, nations can develop because language provides an important link between them and their environment. The use of indigenous languages for promotion of majority participation in aspects of critical concern could have been the position in Zimbabwe since the constitution has promoted 15 indigenous languages to the status of official languages alongside English. Unfortunately, even after such a clear assertion by the national constitution, the sacredness of English has not been altered and still acts as a major obstacle to national development. The position is shared by Magwa (2015) who notes that development in Zimbabwe cannot be achieved without greater utilisation of the indigenous languages in pursuit of scientific economic and social change. African governments, therefore, should ensure that their people have the freedom to express themselves in languages of their choice. It is only after establishing this line of communication and freedom that a populace can be mobilised for engagement in national development. Thus, linguistic imperialism's major blow against post-colonial economies was ensuring the exclusion of the majority by making economic issues discussed in a language they could not freely express themselves in. Instead, even amongst themselves, locals always consider it appropriate for all important issues to be discussed in English even when all the people involved struggle to express themselves in it. It explains why, even after the 2013 declaration on language use, English-only schools are still very popular in the country with the majority only restrained by the unaffordable fees.

Unlike during the colonial era, the decision to ignore all the local languages in favour of English in matters of economic importance is definitely having a negative impact on Zimbabwe's economic development. It means the ruling locals are now trying to run their economy using a foreign language, a condition that Mazrui (1993) says no nation has ever developed in. They have no support from their traditional knowledge systems associated with the language in use which, under normal circumstances, should be the inspiration for most economic developments. This means there is no inspiration for economic development which is the reason the country, just like most African countries, finds it difficult to prosper. In spite of the presence of well-educated economists, businesspeople, engineers and technicians, there is no notable creativity as all efforts being made are attempts to emulate what developed countries have already done. This explains Kishindo's (2000, p. 15) observation that there is no country anywhere in the world (except in Africa) where the most important, most prestigious and most powerful activities of the nation are conducted in what is for most of the citizens a foreign language. The position is further supported by Mazrui's (2002, p. 198) argument that an indigenised approach to national development cannot be complete without great usage of African languages in the pursuit of scientific, artistic and cultural change. He further asserts that Korea, Japan and Malaysia have developed mainly because of the advantage of their own languages.

This study established that the maintenance of the sacredness of English in Zimbabwe over four decades after independence is the major problem with economic development. Efforts still must be made as far as demystifying the perception of the knowledge of English as the only one that opens up economic opportunities in Zimbabwe is concerned. This has made it logical for Africans in the country to continue perceiving knowledge of spoken and written English as more useful and economically rewarding than enhanced knowledge of the local languages and their indigenous languages. This can only be done if the government, as the main employer, starts understanding the nature of linguistic imperialism in the same manner it understands and preaches about political imperialism and national sovereignty. It must understand that political emancipation without linguistic emancipation does not make a country completely free. Once that happens, it can start neutralising the importance of English in favour of the indigenous languages as prescribed by the current constitution. This would allow national policies that avoid victimisation and shunning of job seekers without proficiency in the English language.

The focus group discussants noted that the sacredness attached to English is resulting in a negative attitude towards the indigenous languages. They added that instead of being looked down upon after resorting to the mother tongue, this is making some people opt to remain silent for fear of breaking the English language's grammatical rules even when they have very important viewpoints. One participant confessed that we often hear people saying, 'I wanted to raise this point then you begin to wonder why they remained silent when this could have considerably assisted our discussion'. This is why Gudhlanga (2005) argues that by failing to promote languages and ensuring public participation in matters of national economic interest, the country is losing immensely. She notes that the rural population, which constitutes most of the populace, who rarely possess proficiency in the English language, often find it difficult to secure employment which is the reason they are still very poor over four decades after the attainment of emancipation from colonial rule. Commenting on language attitudes, Kayambazinthu (1998) asserts that it is obvious in social circles that those who know how to speak and write the white man's language have more prestige than those who can only speak African languages. The negative attitude towards the use of African languages in Zimbabwe's ten provinces is representative of many African countries. This is so because, in nearly all the countries, English, the colonial language of 'high culture' and the language of the elite was and is still regarded as the most prestigious language used in parliament, legislature, education, government, science and technology and most academic writings and official correspondences. The colonial language is regarded highly because of the historical processes that put it there and upheld it (Kayambazinthu, 2000, p. 35). The status of English remains what it is because most African governments do not put in place mechanisms for vigorously promoting indigenous languages basically due to failure to understand the real effect of linguistic imperialism.

The decision to continue with the colonial language policy meant the government decided to adopt the former imperial power's approach of treating the multiplicity of indigenous languages as a liability rather than an asset. It could not afford to adopt a different ideology from that of the colonial regime. This meant a decision not to consider the long-term benefits of developing and using indigenous languages in the country. It means the adoption of the colonialist perception of these languages as useless to the country's development. It is very unfortunate that there was no effort to comprehend the implication of the difference between the current administration's relation to the languages as compared to what was the case for the former coloniser. There is no effort to realise that the languages in question mean everything to the local administration in the same way English meant to the colonialists. There is no notable effort to analyse how and why the colonialists prioritised their own language and defended its adoption in the entire country even when only an insignificant group of people spoke it.

The book argues that the position taken by the government on local languages and its impact on the local economy is slowly becoming irreversible. This is so as it is far beyond dispute that the elderly generation who currently act as the custodians of the local languages together with the invaluable indigenous knowledge systems are slowly disappearing through death. They are the only ones who have been lobbying for the recognition of languages and the value associated with them. It leaves the young generation which is generally ignorant and interested in relinquishing all traces of their traditions which they consider medieval and good for nothing, as they were taught to believe by the promoters of linguistic imperialism through education. They have no admiration for the languages and their traditions as they see no value attached to them. The focus group discussants argued that they see only English as the language with the opportunity to open doors for them within the entire global village. This perception of life demonstrates how much they see themselves as nothing more than servants for the developed countries, hence, the crippling brain drain the country constantly battles. They have, thus, been made to fully subscribe to the former coloniser's perception of the multiplicity of indigenous languages as a liability rather than a resource as it derails their mastery of English and, therefore, defeats their ultimate goal in life. It places all the indigenous languages and the traditional knowledge systems they carry, that every developed nation has considered a source of inspiration in their journeys from being developed to developed, in a position where they can never be retrieved. This means a destruction of the only source of the nation's redemption.

A good example, as stated in chapter two, is how the People's Republic of China got totally transformed by the selling of modern medicines developed using Western methods and local herbs housed in the indigenous knowledge systems of the various local languages following the decision to promote local languages. The nation secured itself a slot on the map of developed countries as the entire world saw immense value in these medicines. The same applied to the Japanese whose place on the map of developed countries got ensured by using traditional manure modernised through Western means for mass production of their traditional rice (Mhute & Musingafi, 2015). Instead of recognising such treasures in their indigenous knowledge systems, Zimbabwean languages and cultures are being slowly allowed to vanish with wisdoms. One informant lamented the death of one elderly man who knew a lot of very useful traditional herbs including one which cured all sorts of toothaches without entrusting the knowledge to anyone in this environment where the English method of curing such ailments is by removing teeth is being considered the norm. The development of modern medicines for curing such illnesses could have taken the entire world by surprise earning the nation a lot of money. The chapter argues that, whilst people clearly see the loss of mere indigenous languages through imminent extinction, they must grow to understand that this is facilitating the loss of many invaluable resources attached to them.

Whilst local people see English as an international language ensuring considerable networking within the entire globe, they are not seeing the dependency syndrome introduced by the coloniser that the language is now entrusted to keep alive in their mindset. They are being made to believe and attach all their hopes to a language that is foreign to them. In the same manner, they are made to continue believing solely in foreign economic methods and commodities at the expense of local ones. It is clear evidence of the role of English as a force that was put in place to keep the centre far away from home, a condition no country has ever developed in. This is the reason the government always finds it logical to blame economic challenges being encountered on foreigners' activities such as sanctions, foreign-inspired regime change efforts and the failure of former coloniser to teach locals how to manage the economy after independence. Whilst the value of networking can never be underscored, excessive trust for and reliance on the external world is dangerous. It destroys the necessary belief in local opportunities and capabilities which creates room for abuse and exploitation. For instance, a lot of incidences are being reported of people being abused in foreign countries as they get trapped into slavery under the pretext of getting employed overseas. For example, on 12 March 2022, *Zimbabwe Observer* published a story entitled '100 Zimbabwean women sexually abused and treated as slaves in Oman'. The story has it that the women were stranded in Oman after being trafficked to the Middle East country on false job promises. According to the publication, Aaron Nhepera, the Secretary for Home Affairs, had told the media that 18 cases had already been reported. Such cases are on the rise with some

Zimbabwean nurses being reported as failing to make ends meet in developed countries like England after being assisted with flight costs by agents who are now taking almost all of their earnings. It shows that in as much as networking through English is promoting employment opportunities abroad, it has also lessened the desire in many people to believe in their capabilities in developing their own local economic solutions for their problems resulting in considerable cases of abuse. In fact, we can choose to argue that locals have become international beggars for them to survive. The nation is also benefiting from the development as its diaspora remittances are rising significantly. For instance, the *Economist Intelligence* of 6 May 2o21 published an article entitled 'Zimbabwean Remittances Soar' which indicates that on 4 May, Zimbabwe's finance minister, Professor Mthuli Ncube, announced that remittances from the diaspora reached some US$1bn in 2020, compared with US636m in 2019 (www.country.euiu.com/article.aspx?). Two things can be deduced from the announcement. The first one is a significant rise in the number of people whose needs the nation is failing to cater for resulting in sorting for foreign assistance. Second, though tough for me as a patriotic national to say, this can be considered an instance of our sovereign nation proudly enjoying the revenue from its citizenry's begging activities within the global market.

Conclusion

The chapter has demonstrated how much linguistic imperialism influenced economic progress in Southern Rhodesia. It indicates that the promotion of English and the demotion of all indigenous languages to insignificant entities went a long way in promoting the success of an economy that was centred on native English speakers using traditional English economic systems in an environment with enhanced resources like fertile land, minerals and cheap labour. This facilitated the transformation of the nation that used to be characterised by disgruntled warring kingdoms into a significant economic base within the region that served as the breadbasket of the region up to a decade or so after the attainment of independence. The chapter, however, proceeds to demonstrate how the adoption of the same linguistic configuration after independence proves futile for the Zimbabweans' economic endeavours despite having adopted the same economic policies. Even efforts to withdraw farmlands, mines and industries from the whites who were believed to be saboteurs of the nation's economy could not bail out the situation. This proves that the correct recipe is always when the nation is run by people using their native languages with proper importance accorded to their local traditional wisdom, with foreign ones coming in to modify what is already there. The following chapter focuses on the effect of linguistic imperialism on the sociocultural aspects of the country during and after independence.

5 Sociocultural Impact of the Rhodesian and Zimbabwean Language Policies

Introduction

Having dwelled considerably on the economic effects of linguistic imperialism in the preceding chapter, this chapter is set to assess the sociocultural effects. Considering the inseparability of language and culture, it tries to stress the true nature of linguistic imperialism's influence during and after colonisation by unpacking the joys and troubles experienced in Southern Rhodesian and Zimbabwean sociocultural environments due to the adopted linguistic parameters. It assesses the extent to which the colonialists' Social Darwinist perception of themselves as the ones at an advanced level of the evolution ladder, and, thus, mandated to usher civilisation and development to the unenlightened ones (Mike, 1997), has been confirmed through the linguistic arrangements. Efforts are made in the process, for instance, to demonstrate how the linguistically inspired dependency syndrome has inspired national efforts to shun everything typical of the local traditions regardless of the possible benefits that are being enjoyed by some first world countries.

Defining Culture

Culture has been summarily seen as the totality of a people's way of life. It is the sum of the ways through which a community conquers the challenges of its environment. In this regard, it is the existence and metaphysics of their being and includes the customs, beliefs, art, music and all other products of human thought typical of a particular group of people at a particular time (Umeogu & Ifeoma, 2012). It is the actual aspect that distinguishes one society from another, or a kind of identification which, when exhibited, reveals or gives an inkling of where you came from. For instance, a mode of dressing often leads to such comments like 'you dress like an African' in the same way it can result in others like 'you look like you are coming from the airport'.

Sociocultural Effects of Southern Rhodesian Language Choices

I have already highlighted the white settler government's desire to generate another home away from their real home, and to achieve this goal, they made stern efforts to promote the English language to the highest level in the territory. This has been confirmed by Ngara (1982, p. 24) who notes that during colonial Southern Rhodesia 'the belief that English was a superior language to Shona (an African language) was made clearly visible'. Together with the language, the settlers were also eager to generate a society practising the Western lifestyle in its totality. In this regard, they had to ensure a considerable size of the native English community to make sure the typical lifestyle is permanently ensured. The development was also believed to enhance the locals' learning of the language and lifestyle in line with the argument that native-like fluency in a second language requires exposure to a society practising both the target society's language and culture. This resulted in the introduction of incentives to lure as many native English speakers as possible to the new territory. As indicated by the focus group discussants, this ushered in efforts to facilitate the English lifestyle on the land, chief amongst them being the demotion of all local languages to a status of insignificance.

In line with the foregoing, the white settler imposed English as the language of conquest, and the empire slowly formed a linguistic basis for the creation of an indigenous elite who devalued indigenous languages. This was done to wipe out traces of the local languages together with the sociocultural practices they carried which the intruder decided to castigate as medieval, evil and overdue for extinction. It saw the introduction of the so-called modern Western lifestyle in the form of dressing, speaking and perception of reality, amongst others. For instance, this fuelled the desire for money to meet the new standard of living and, thus, facilitated the need to offer very cheap labour in farms, mines and industries, thereby sustaining their economic imperialism. It made every one of the locals aspire to speak the high-status language and practise the high-status lifestyle that goes with it as it was the only gateway to better treatment, especially in the workplaces.

In this regard, whilst the colonial era is popularly known for its harsh treatment of most of the locals resulting in names like *vadzvanyiriri* (oppressors) and *vasvetasimba* (parasites), the fortunate ones who quickly earned proficiency in the English language got the opportunity to join some kind of middle class between whites and locals and were assured of much better treatment. The focus group discussants scoffed at how the ability to speak English and dress like the white people got rewarded by some unusual access to restricted areas and services like walking in Harare's first street and drinking clear beer. This immensely heightened the urge to join this class that, even over four decades after independence, locals still take a lot of pride in their as well as their offsprings' ability to emulate the native English lifestyle. This proves how the settler government went miles to incentivise the locals' desire to emulate them. Those who could show ability to dress, speak or eat like the white men were even praised by locals within the entire society. A good example is that of the usual admiration for how English was spoken by the elderly who did standard six during the colonial era and those who used to work in white people's houses. This meant a celebration of the ability of locals to look down upon their selves and move away from their typical cultures and identities. It meant heroism for self-hate and the promotion of the white man to a model of the entire society, a position that still exists in most locals' minds.

Religion

The white settlers' decision to popularise their native language to suppress all local ones worked considerably well for all other sociocultural aspects of the society linked to it. Religion is one such aspect where foreigners got a chance to totally establish themselves at the expense of the locals. In the then Southern Rhodesia, the local traditional religion became a major target for the settler government due to the pivotal role it played in the 1896 to 1897 uprising by the Shona and the Ndebele which people popularly tagged as the First Chimurenga. The name Chimurenga itself was derived from Murenga the popular spirit medium considered to be the founder ancestor of Zimbabwe. Apart from the role played by Murenga, other spirit mediums' role was overwhelming. For instance, Nehanda's assistance even rendered guns ineffective against the Shona for some time until information about the herb behind the development got leaked, courtesy of locals who were eager to attain the white man's favour. However, with the defeat, the local population was considerably disillusioned at the failure of a rebellion which had been undertaken at the bidding of the ancestral spirits from. Consequently, some began to doubt the power of the spirits, they had traditionally worshipped and began to turn to foreign religions. In addition to this, the white settler government had not been very surprised by the rebellion of the Ndebele in 1893 but they had not expected the kind of armed resistance from the Shona. After realising the role of the spirit mediums in the effort, they were more determined than ever to make the victory more prosperous and successful (Coleman et al., 1983). They began to make an exercise of weakening the tribal beliefs and customs, chief amongst which was the further relegation of the indigenous languages that carried them. This, together with the incentives for practising the Western lifestyle, successfully lured a lot of local Zimbabweans to foreign religions over the years.

Christianity is one such religion that conquered almost every one of the local blacks. Through it, the local African traditional religion was demonised as medieval, evil and keeping believers stuck in darkness with the practices associated with it being considered completely barbaric. This is why, for instance, despite the Bible being silent about Western processed tree and herbal medicines in hospitals, unprocessed traditional medicines from similar trees and herbs were castigated by Christianity as evil (until recently when only two or so apostolic sects with origins in Zimbabwe started a move against the Western ones too as they proscribe members from going to hospitals). As such, it became very shameful to associate oneself with the traditional religion. Contrarily, Christianity became the norm for most of the country, and the introduction and establishment of a foreign language and sociocultural aspects related to it were the main weapon. This signalled a complete conquest of the local cultures and the languages that carried them.

Health

It should be noted that the defeat of the Shona and Ndebele people in the 1896 to 1897 uprising was a major blow to the local culture. Colonialists embarked on destroying the indigenous identity through the imposition of the English language as 'the language'. This saw the waging of some kind of linguistic terrorism to make all indigenous cultures fossil. This is captured by Ndlovu-Gatsheni (2020, p. 1) who argues that colonialism resulted in epistemicide (where you kill and displace pre-existing knowledges), linguicide (killing and displacing the languages of a people and imposing your own) and culturecide (where you kill or replace the cultures of a people). Thus, colonialism turned both languages and the cultures they carried fossil with the minority languages and their cultures being affected the most. This is the reason Prah (2002, p. 76) notes that 'colonialism triumphed through the perpetration of various degrees of ethnocide by condemning indigenous languages and cultures as inferior and irredeemably primitive'. Thus, colonialists perpetrated various magnitudes of ethnocide by condemning indigenous languages and cultures as irredeemably inferior and medieval.

Acceptance of the supremacy of the English language in the country brought about belief in the white man and his culture. This meant recognition of that culture as the solution to all types of problems and one such is health challenges. The coloniser publicised his approach to health challenges as the only logical and effective one. Hospitals and clinics were availed and people's access to the services was initially free of charge to lure the entire populace to it. Efforts were also made to castigate the locals' traditional ways of dealing with the illnesses to ensure an end to their self-reliance and create a gap that would always ensure the white man's relevance. For instance, the traditional healer (*n'anga*) was referred to as a witch doctor, a term meant to denigrate the profession. Whilst this made most progressive locals avoid thinking twice before moving away from sorting for their services, it drew them closer to the Western ways. In a way, it indirectly forced them to look down upon themselves and their usual beliefs at the same time forcing them to acknowledge the foreigners as agents of progress and development who had come to redeem them from darkness. Whereas it worked well for the coloniser, the locals got some access to medical services that were not available in their communities. For instance, pregnancy complications and mending of broken bones were ensured without much trouble.

Linguistic Imperialism's Impact on Zimbabwean Sociocultural Aspects

People perceived colonialism as the sole aspect that displaced the local languages and the sociocultural norms and values they carry. In that regard, one would logically expect the attainment of independence to usher in the lost respect for indigenous languages together with the sociocultural practices typical of the land. Unfortunately, as indicated in the previous chapters, efforts were made by the new government to ensure continuity by carrying on with the colonial legacy as far as language use is concerned. This is because the post-colonial language policy in Zimbabwe has not shifted considerably from the colonial one (Gudhlanga, 2005). It is regrettably so although appertaining to language and culture, the Constitution of Zimbabwe Amendment (No.20) Act 2013 section 63 clearly avers the following:

Every person has the right:

(a) to use the language of their choice;
(b) to participate in the cultural life of their choice.

Whilst it clearly states that all institutions and agencies of government must, at every level, ensure that all the 16 officially recognised languages are treated equitably and the state must promote and advance the use of all languages used in Zimbabwe, including sign language, and must create conditions for the development of those languages, the country still advances the politics of language in which English is dominating. In other words, in practice, the colonial approach to local languages remains the order of the day which confirms the observation that the government was just strategically silencing the pressure from language committees and pressure groups within the country. This keeps threatening the existence of all indigenous languages together with the sociocultural aspects they carry.

Indigenous Language Use

Although English has remained the language for official communication, some improvement in indigenous language use in Zimbabwe could be noted. Chimhundu (1993) observes the use of some of the so-called minority languages in programmes on local radio stations. This was boosted further by the 75% local content that was introduced in 2005, though this was primarily meant to generate more audience for the ruling political party (ZANU

PF) propaganda with adverts for its land reform programmes such as '*rambai makashinga*' (stay strong) being aired after every 5 minutes on all local radios. This was captured by Gudhlanga (2005) as well who applauded the considerable increase in the use of indigenous languages in the electronic media with almost every one of the six official minority languages having some airtime in the various TV and Radio stations in addition to Shona and Ndebele. Gudhlanga also observes how quite several agricultural and cultural programmes were being aired in Shona and Ndebele. She noted the significant increase in the screening of comedies in both Shona and Ndebele, the popular ones being *Parafini, Gringo* and *Bhonzo nechikwata*. Zimbabwean movies, *Neria* and *Yellow Card* which were produced in English, were also quickly translated into Shona and Ndebele. Of note are also efforts by the Department of African Languages and Literature of the University of Zimbabwe which started an African Languages Lexical (ALLEX) project in 1992 which later developed into the African Languages Research Institute (ALRI) in 2000. As Chimhundu (1999) says, the programme was dedicated to research and development of African languages in Zimbabwe. Recently, one such institute has been introduced under the Midlands State University as well.

However, it is unfortunate still that the safety of Zimbabwean indigenous languages is still highly threatened by the promotion of English. ALRI, for instance, has already died a natural death with its workers being incorporated under the University's Language, Literature and Culture Studies department. The focus group discussants noted with great concern how many of the degree programmes in indigenous languages are struggling to yield viable classes in most universities, a condition that has fuelled the decision to merge the traditional department of African Languages and Literature with others like Linguistics, and English and Communication throughout the state universities. An explanation for this is provided by Chimhundu (1993, p. 58) who observes that, in the current post-colonial era in Zimbabwe, there is an unbalanced bi-cultural and bilingual situation in which the High status or H language is the official language of the former colonial power, whilst the indigenous languages are the Low status or L languages. It means that African languages, such as Shona and Ndebele, are looked down upon as less important socially and culturally in Zimbabwean society. This is all because the promotion of the English language paved the ground for the permanent accommodation of its native speakers' culture. As a result, just like in the colonial era, in post-colonial Zimbabwe, the white settlers are still idolised by many locals as being endowed with unalienable supernatural ways of doing things. The focus group discussants even highlighted how much local people are always nostalgic for the coloniser's principledness, leadership and training, amongst other things. Speaking, dressing and even behaving like the colonial master have become the most cherished ways. This is the reason the ability to code mix and switch to English often guarantees a lot of respect from fellow locals even to this day throughout Zimbabwe. An informant observed with great concern how, even in meetings where people are free to use a language of their choice, people tend to ignore valid points expressed in local languages only for someone to attain credit for repeating them in English. Similarly, nose brigades became a very popular way after independence for nasalising their entire speeches to sound more like native English speakers.

This attitude towards English impacted heavily on the desire to speak indigenous languages in the country. Bhabha (1984) argues that the colonised usually mimic their masters. This desire of members of the colonised society to imitate and take on the culture of the colonisers confirms 'the desire for a reformed, recognizable Other' (Bhabha, 1984, p. 126). Magwa (2015) notes that Zimbabwe is one of the many African countries that continues to take pride in the use of a foreign language as its primary media of communication at the expense of local ones. This is in spite of the fact that the country has Shona, a language spoken by almost 85% of the population (Hachipola, 1998). The Shona and Ndebele people living in Zimbabwe have been denied the advantage of utilising their indigenous languages in matters of national development and this is having dire effects on the society. Umeogu and Ifeoma (2012) argue that an example of the elimination of epistemology is such replacement of African languages with European ones. According to them, it is a shame, for example, that a boy cannot understand a simple question in his mother tongue. When he grows up with the ideology that vernacular is inferior, he would not be able to teach his children because one cannot give what they do not have. There are also efforts by Zimbabwean parents, as the focus group discussants stressed, to detach themselves as much as possible from the indigenous languages and the cultures they carry for the sake of bringing their offspring closer to English even decades after independence. One of them brought to the foe the issue of some parents who go to the extent of sending their children to former A schools (currently being tagged as English-only schools) and employing maids proficient in English to minimise their children's exposure to indigenous languages and cultures. This has left most of the indigenous languages with only limited elders who can speak them which is a clear sign of impending language death. This is in line with Fishman (2000) who postulates that language loss proceeds through eight stages, with stage eight being the closest to complete extinction. He summarises the stages as follows: Stage 1: Some language use in higher level educational, occupational, governmental and media efforts, but without the additional safety provided by political independence. Stage 2: Language is used by the local government and in the mass media in the minority community. Stage 3: Language is used in places of business and by employees in less specialised work areas. Stage 4: Language is required in elementary schools. Stage 5: Language is still very much alive and used in the home and community, but there is no reinforcement besides the community itself. Stage 6: Some intergenerational use of language. Stage 7: Only adults beyond childbearing age speak the language. Stage 8: Only a few elderly people speak the language.

The foregoing confirms Magwa's (2015) assertion that whilst in 1996 UNESCO went as far as proclaiming the Universal Declaration on Linguistic Rights, which requests that national and supernational authorities accept their responsibility for the preservation and development of the world's languages and for the introduction of binding legislation within this field, due to linguistic imperialism, the owners of the indigenous languages themselves are eager to free themselves from the languages' traces for good. This is why it is often argued that linguistic imperialism dovetails with all other types of imperialism and is an integral part of them and the reason Phillipson (1992) argues that linguistic imperialism is a component of cultural imperialism. Thus, clarifying how the English language has accorded great value to everything associated with its culture in Zimbabwe, thereby proving that language and culture are inseparable. This is why Ngugi (1986) says language has a dual character as it is both a means of communication and a carrier of culture. In other words, it is a medium of interaction with society as well as a repository of a people's culture, values aspirations and beliefs. Language is, therefore, one of the indispensable features of the cultural systems of all societies and it penetrates all aspects of social and cultural spheres.

Due to the negative attitude towards indigenous languages, Zimbabweans sometimes feel amused or even embarrassed when a native language is spoken in a very official context. An informant noted that 'people who decide to use indigenous languages in offices, even when all participants are comfortable with the local language, are usually reminded accordingly, "Tava kumusha here?"' (Are we at home?). This would be a polite way of restricting the use of the indigenous languages even at a time the constitution has placed fifteen of the indigenous languages at the same level as English in the country. All this is happening even when Anyidoho (1992), Ngugi (1987) and Uju (2008) consider language a liberating force for its speakers if it is empowered. This confirms that whereas cultural diversity, which encompasses protection and preservation of indigenous languages, was boldly stated, the implementation of the 2013 constitution linguistic framework was cosmetic as the use of indigenous languages has remained restricted whilst the recognition of minority languages such as Chibarwe, Kalanga, Khoisan, Nambya, Ndau, Shangani, Sotho, Tonga, Tswana, Venda and Xhosa is just theoretical. Minority languages continue to be marginalised based on ethnicity. Ethnicity, in this context, refers to a cultural-oriented concept centred on norms, values, beliefs and practices. All this results from the seeds strategically sowed through linguistic imperialism and considering the possibility of a number of the languages dying in the near future, I can confidently argue that the Zimbabwean approach to language use is advancing the Rhodesian linguistic agenda to a level where returning is impossible.

Cultural Dependency

Cultural dependency is a situation when a country is controlled by another as the dominant one puts pressure on the other to adopt its culture, values and lifestyle. It dwells upon the existence of some form of inequality amongst the partners involved. English usage in Zimbabwe has made the ground quite uneven for the indigenous culture in Zimbabwe and minority languages were hit the hardest. Ndlovu-Gatsheni (2020, p. 1) argues that we cannot stress fully the suppression of indigenous languages through the promotion of English without highlighting the effect on minority languages. This has also been captured by Chimhundu (2002) who says colonialism led to the marginalisation of indigenous languages, especially those of minority ethnic groups. All these local groups have been made to depend solely on the higher culture. To demonstrate this, the following aspects illustrate the rampant dependency syndrome.

Religion

The number of Christians in Zimbabwe increased immensely after independence as many more churches and religions emerged. This has left only an insignificant fraction of the locals linked to the local traditional religion. Focus group discussants even argued that the African traditional religion is as good as dead in Zimbabwe further noting how people often go to Mozambique should they encounter challenges requiring such assistance. One of the informants argued that

> *'Zimbabwe can now be considered a Christian nation with only pockets of Muslims and local traditional believers'.*

This reliance on foreign religions is traceable to efforts of the settler government to promote the English language and culture. The progression of the threats to local religions, just like any other customs and norms, demonstrates the impact linguistic imperialism continues to have in the country even over four decades after independence.

It is critical to indicate that evidence of the degree to which Christianity has conquered the entire Zimbabwean nation could be attained from how much it has taken prominent figures like former President Robert Gabriel Mugabe and President Mnangagwa on board. The special connection between the nation's presidium and Christian churches is quite evident and often publicised in mainstream media. Apart from many Christian churches emerging, the nation has also seen other foreign religions like Islam coming in and taking considerable numbers from the national followers with another informant even going further by pointing at Satanism as another emerging competitor. All this is happening at the expense of traditional religion which has come to be almost completely associated with evil things, especially with foreign churches' tendency of associating traditional healers with evil practices like producing and selling of goblins that later turn against and wipe their owners' families. Very few (if any) locals still consider identifying themselves with the religion, even after many traditional healers like Chipinge's late Ndunge managed to get so popular with prominent church leaders and prophets. It is a clear sign of defeat for the traditional belief system, the local culture it is part of as well as the language carrying it. With culture being a part of the community's identity, this demonstrates a huge success in the former coloniser's endeavour to alienate the locals from themselves.

Health

Another sector that is being significantly impacted by the colonialist-inspired migration to the English language and culture is that of health. The informants observed that, due to the Southern Rhodesian language policy, after independence more efforts are being made to embrace the English lifestyle together with all its sociocultural practices in the name of modernity. Whilst cultures and their traditions are a people's priceless intangible heritage, both national and minority language cultures were abandoned in favour of the English ones. A lot was obviously lost in the form of the traditional knowledge systems as the young ones became unprepared to associate themselves with those aspects of languages considered useless, backward and even barbaric. They are not prepared to allow their elders' knowledge systems to be passed on to them as they have been tagged as anti-Christian. As such, most of the elderly are passing away with priceless knowledge entrusted to them by their elders like traditional medicines. The interviewees highlighted with great concern that only the limited fortunate families are 'those whose members got informed about such information in their dreams by their departed elders'. This demonstrates how much of the intangible resources the country has lost together with the relegation of the languages.

The promotion of English and its culture also brought a major transformation in the health section since the colonial era. Whilst the culture carried by the local languages emphasised traditional healers' services who relied on the local herbs for the treatment of various illnesses, English ushered in a culture where health issues were attended to in hospitals by nurses and doctors using Western medicines. Whilst the local health services were traditionally the responsibility of possessed practitioners, nowadays nurses and doctors are being educated on all health issues. The foreign approach has been adopted and popularised within the local community as well. This has seen education and health institutions being built across the country. Complete faith has been entrusted to this approach to health issues across the country with only very few still moving back and forth as far as embracing it is concerned.

I have considerably explained how linguistic imperialism facilitated a shift from a traditional to an English health system. Rasmussen (1979, p. 113) has it that 'through independence, Zimbabwe had one of the highest standards of health of any country in Africa which enhanced the potential of the highest possible health system in the region but never materialised'. This is because the instilled faith in a foreign language as well as the foreign healthcare system typical of it did not become an end in itself. Rather, it bred continuous faith in foreign systems at the expense of local ones. As a result, instead of developing the local hospitals and clinics and equipping them with the best possible facilities, the government officials and the rich in Zimbabwe kept their faith in medical care services on foreign lands. The nation seems to have been totally robbed of its ability to have faith in anything local. To this date, government officials and those who are rich opt for flying to foreign countries within and outside the continent even for their routine medical check-ups. This is having dire effects on most of the populace who, in cases of more challenging illnesses like those involving the heart, have to call for donations to access foreign facilities as well since the government feels no obligation to have the advanced facilities locally. Informants lamented how, in such cases, unlucky ones who fail to raise huge sums of money are left with no chance of survival. Thus, the settler government's efforts to abolish belief in indigenous languages in favour of English (a foreign one) are having far-reaching effects on the local populace even decades after the attainment of independence.

Eating Habits

Another area that got heavily affected by the culture dependency that was ushered in by linguistic imperialism is that of eating habits. As people are trying their best to embrace English, they are making stern efforts to embrace the foods typical of the English culture. They are trying their best to abandon the traditional foods for the foreign ones and the reason food outlets are in English even where the target customers are locals more comfortable with local languages. The informants observed that not many families still have any traces of traditional foods in their diets at a time a considerable number of exotic foods have become infamous for causing chronic diseases like diabetes, hypertension and cancer which traditionally were never heard of. It is no longer a secret that ageing, teeth, back and even eye problems have since increased (especially in young people) due to the food habits that came with the English language. Surprisingly, health practitioners are even advocating for the consumption of traditional stuff like small grains, vegetables and fruits to mitigate some of the effects of these exotic foods. Similarly, to minimise the rampant food-related problems, traditional ways of preparing food are also being encouraged by the health personnel, such as boiling vegetables and meat instead of frying as well as using peanut butter instead of cooking oil or margarine. The same is being said about using traditional clay pots rather than the Western pots that have conquered every corner of our society. Unfortunately, the majority of the local populace cannot stand such foods and ways of preparing them even if they happen to be specifically prescribed to do so by health practitioners in cases of sickness. An informant alluded to how, to some, this often appears like a real punishment. It confirms the degree of alienation as the local populace could neither stand being separated from English and its lifestyle nor being reunited with the indigenous languages and their traditional lifestyles even at a time Western health specialists are recommending it. This is a clear indication of the damage linguistic imperialism has inflicted on the country through the presentation of English and its lifestyle as the high status one. The informants lamented the efforts that were undertaken, especially during the first decades of Zimbabwean independence to replace traditional crops with foreign ones, and traditional trees (even fruit bearing ones) with exotic trees like gumtree and jacaranda. It proved that linguistic imperialism had completed the task by the time the country gained independence as the seed had already been sown.

Death of Hunhu/Ubuntu Philosophy

The level of alienation of the citizens from the traditional *Hunhu/Unhu/ Ubuntu* philosophy that is typical of the Bantu cultures is quite critical in demonstrating the impact of the colonial and post-colonial language policies in Zimbabwe. Mabvurira (2020) refers to philosophy as an African moral theory associated with humanness. It is pervasive in all parts of the African continent as demonstrated by the fact that the meanings and principles of *Ubuntu* are similar across all the African languages (Broodryk, 2005). The word *Ubuntu* itself is derived from Bantu languages of Africa, hence, it is an African philosophy. Furtherance to this, all Africans share this common *Ubuntu* ideology (Samkange & Samkange, 1980) which makes it conceptualised as a symbol of African identity. This is the reason Mabvurira (2020) argues that the *Ubuntu* philosophy is one of the supreme contributions of the peoples of Africa to the entire world.

The philosophy states that a typical person upholds proper or typical sociocultural norms and values centred on the promotion of love as well as communality. This gives rise to the assertions like 'I am because we are', 'I am human because I belong' and 'a person is a person because of or through others' (Moloketi, 2009; Tutu, 2004). It is also the reason behind Mugumbate and Nyanguru's (2013) argument that *Ubuntu* is the basis of the African communal cultural life as well as Mazrui's (2001) assertion that Ubuntu is distinctive for its short memory of hate. Thus, it expresses interconnectedness, common humanity and responsibility to others (Koster, 1996; Nussbaum, 2003) and under it, communities are socioculturally bound (Mangaliso, 2001; Prinsloo, 2000). Unfortunately, efforts by the colonialist to destroy the indigenous languages in post-colonial Zimbabwe and many other African societies have destroyed the philosophy. Together with English language, individualism, which is the opposite of Ubuntu and associated with Western societies, has become the order of the day with the nation becoming infamous for many inhuman practices. The *Hunhu/Ubuntu* solidarity that typically eliminates hunger, isolation, deprivation, poverty and individualism is no more. Respect for the brotherly and sisterly concern for humanity, cooperation, care and sharing that is typical of *Hunhu/Ubuntu* that ensures societal rather than individual benefit is no more too. Our society's atypical deviation from the philosophy is also the explanation for the rampant heinous acts like rape, child marriages, human trafficking, incestuous activities, etc.

Violence perpetrated by the political parties in the country is another pointer to the level of loss of *Hunhu* to which the country has unfortunately stooped. The Catholic Commission of Justice and Peace and the Legal Resources Foundation Report (1997, p. 70) has it that 'one of the worst cases of dissident violence took place immediately after the election in August 1985, in the Mwenezi District of southern Zimbabwe. Here 17 Shona-speaking villagers, including small children, were murdered by dissidents, allegedly for voting for ZANU-PF in the elections. Thirty-five people were herded into a hut and the Ndebele speakers were then allowed to leave. The rest of the people were shot at, and the hut was set on fire. As survivors tried to escape, they were shot, including two-year-olds. The dissidents then went on to loot a nearby store and killed a further five people, bringing the total number murdered that day to twenty-two'. This demonstrates that instead of the settlers' perception of blacks as animals who could even be killed at will being discarded at independence, it has been inherited by the black locals, and all this can be attributed to linguistic imperialism that uprooted the Hunhu philosophy that used to promote unconditional respect for humanity.

For another logical example, Raftopolous (2009, p. 229) posits that, in the 2008 general elections that brought Mugabe of ZANU PF and Tsvangirai of MDC head-to-head, the latter proved to be the partial victor after he pulled 47.9% of the votes whilst the former managed 41.2% of the same. What this result proved was the fact that Tsvangirai was more popular at that time compared to Mugabe, a political statement that did not go all the way in paving an electoral victory for Morgan Richard Tsvangirai. The Constitution directed that for one to be declared President of the country, one should draw 50% plus one of the total votes. The obtaining scenario called for a run-off. Raftopolous (2009, p, 229) succinctly unpacks the run-off saying 'it was, however, the violence that preceded the presidential run-off at the end of June that played the country into further political uncertainty. The violence inflicted by the ruling party on the electorate as punishment for its loss in the March election and as warning against the repeat of such a vote, was the worst seen in the country since the Gukurahundi massacres of the mid-1980s'. One focus group discussant alluded to how

> '*people were asked to either chose death or have their body parts (hands and legs) amputated. Should you choose the latter, you would be asked if you preferred a short (leg or hand) or long*'.

Another informant attributed the many mentally unstable people who surfaced immediately after the run-off to their being hounded by the spirits of the people they killed at the time. At the centre of it all is the uncalled-for political excesses for which, as reported by Raftopolous, violence is deployed as a means and tool to cow the masses into electoral submission and acquiescence.

Corruption is another major pointer to the extent to which Hunhu has been buried together with the marginalisation of indigenous languages in the country. Under Hunhuism, people cannot afford to put their own benefits and happiness before that of the entire community but rather find their individual satisfaction in the ultimate happiness of their entire society. In such a society, there is no room for the kind of corruption that has come to characterise even the top brass of the country's government. A very good example is the Willogate and Willowvale Scandals which saw high-ranking ministers being accused of putrid corruption. The names Maurice Nyagumbo, Enos Nkala and Kumbirai Kangai fall into this cohort. It was now black on black, thus pointing to the crude reality that ugliness, be it political, economic and/or social, is an inherent human trait that should never be aligned to race, creed, skin pigmentation or any other prejudice. Another typical example is how the 2017 coup in the country arguably focused solely on removing the criminals around the then President Robert Gabriel Mugabe, and the main crime most of them had committed was misuse of office through corrupt actions. The fact that even those victims accused of fraudulent practices involving millions of dollars were out roaming freely immediately after their arrest shows the degree of corruption within the country due to the English-related individualism that replaced our typical Ubuntu philosophy.

Appearance and Lifestyle

As already highlighted, linguistic imperialism is having a great impact on sociocultural imperialism because culture is transmitted from generation to generation through language. As such, shifting towards facilitating English language acquisition instead of indigenous ones promoted the effective replacement of indigenous norms, values and all other social practices with English ones. This is why dressing, for instance, has been significantly impacted on in Zimbabwe. Western ways of dressing have become the norm and as highlighted in the focus group discussions,

> *'only an insignificant fraction of the locals still know what the Zimbabwean traditional dressing looks like'.*

Local women who used to be custodians of local morals and values are now associated with Western clothes like trousers and miniskirts which used to be popularly considered indecent in the country. Whilst initially these were associated with English women and later with locals who used to migrate to work as prostitutes in urban areas, they have now become the most typical attire for all local women. An informant went to the extent of stressing how difficult it has become to come across women whose wardrobes have even a single dress that the locals would consider decent.

In terms of appearance, instead of the usual black Zimbabwean beauty, English has ushered in a situation where light colour has become synonymous with beauty. Whilst during the colonial era there used to be Ambit and one or two creams for lightening skins, nowadays more inventions are coming on board in the form of creams, soaps, injections and face powders. These include products like depresone, movert, doctor clear, skin doctor, lemon light, light up and gentle magic, most of which have become infamous for unbearable side effects including skin cancer. The increase in variety demonstrates the growing interest in lightening the skin as well as market size. The focus group discussants agreed that it has become quite difficult to find affording women who do not use them. In the same vein, they indicated that short or natural hair has become a sign of poverty whilst lengthened hair has become the norm for almost all affording women. Braids, weaves and wigs are some common examples with some even getting to the extent of dying their straightened hair or making locks using other people's hair just for them to look like the native English speakers. Thus, through language, the coloniser has successfully alienated the locals from their own selves forever, since instead of thinking of its reversal after independence, the condition is getting much worse with time. All of it serves to demonstrate that, instead of colonial torture and atrocities of the liberation struggle generating hatred for the perpetrator, linguistic imperialism has sown undying love for the native English speaker and their looks. It no longer appears as if they snatched everything that was rightfully theirs.

To further demonstrate how the perception of our selves has been impacted by the transition to English and the culture associated with it, beauty is now perceived from the Western perspective. Instead of the utility beauty, like the *mutsikapanotinhira or chigagairwa* (heavy weights), who were traditionally considered beautiful as they were associated with the power necessary for undertaking a variety of important tasks, people are now judged with Western lenses in which the slim ones are perceived as the best. To demonstrate the seriousness of the matter, ladies often diet to the extent of starving themselves and keep exercising to keep their weight down. Body shapes are also being assessed from a Western point of view which has seen some locals going as far as taking pills and injections, some of which with dire side effects, to alter their usual appearances. The main physical alterations pursued include big breasts, big backs and big hips. Focus group discussants have scoffed at how often they come across people whose two hips are of notably different sizes. Informants lamented as well how the desire for an opportunity to access the expensive 'beautifying' commodities has led many young girls into unnecessary relationships or even the streets to practise prostitution. Some of the school-going girls are not spared in this with some getting to the extent of going for sugar dads to fund the luxuries and the reason diseases like AIDS have had the better part of the society.

It is critical to stress that the growing love for material things that came with the foreign language and culture has immensely boosted the desire for money as this lifestyle is quite expensive. It has also kept the influence of the former imperial power necessary as the people cannot resist the urge to import clothes and all other necessities for use in emulating their physical beings and lifestyles. This confirms the fact that, through linguistic imperialism, the imperial power strategically implemented parameters that would make them relevant forever and no wonder why they are considerably involved in manufacturing the creams, powders and injections locals often go for to alter their looks.

The desire for the English lifestyle and the greediness for the Western wealth that could secure it are quite alarming as it has many going to the extent of shamelessly practicing despicable acts like murdering and raping their own children and other dearest relatives. This demonstrates how the locals have run away from their usual selves which used to believe in nothing other than typical norms such as collectivity, solidarity, acceptance, dignity and hospitality (Mbigi & Maree, 1997). Rather, they have fallen for a foreign philosophy that gives rise to individualism which in turn fuels selfishness, greediness, corruption and lack of respect for life and typical African norms and values. Thus, they now aspire to totally emulate the Western mindset that is aptly expressed in Descartes', 'I think, therefore, I am', which is the most succinct expression of the basis of Western individualism (Hapanyengwi-Chemhuru & Makuvaza, 2014, p. 3).

Local relationships which used to be based on Unhu/Ubuntu principles have significantly been transformed towards English ones as well. Informants observed how the respect that used to be typical of in-laws has since been castigated as backward. The sacredness of such relationships, which used to ensure the decency necessary for a peaceful society, has since been scrapped. This has now seen people advocating for freedom of association with totems that used to bind relatives being perceived as medieval and useless. People of similar totems are now marrying whilst atypical cases of in-laws and siblings impregnating each other are on the rise. Others are going to the extent of exercising same-sex marriages and even advocating for its recognition by the constitution as is the case in some Western countries.

Conclusion

As Umeogu and Ifeoma (2012) have rightly noted, all the time and money spent on the Independence Day celebration is being wasted as we are more of slaves that are being made to celebrate freedom whilst still bound in slavery. Linguistic imperialism has successfully placed us in a situation where we can hardly get rid of our colonial bondage and one way through which it ensures this is by making our society's desire for sociocultural transformation towards the former imperial power and their sociocultural practices irresistible. Even over 40 years after independence, the people are increasingly idolising the former coloniser's looks, perception and way of life. Efforts are still being made to emulate their ways of survival and appearance as much as possible in spite of all the efforts that have been made to talk about the desire to relinquish their influence and emancipate ourselves from their clutches. We need all that is typical of them when on the surface we claim to be totally against them for the suffering they inflicted upon us over the years. The chapter demonstrated how efforts to fully liberate ourselves would always be fruitless as the adopted language policies act like some remote control meant to advance the motives of the former coloniser within the society. All this has been and is still being ensured in the name of modernity, development or progress.

6 Educational Effects of Rhodesian and Zimbabwean Language Policies

Introduction

Having demonstrated the huge effect of linguistic imperialism on the sociocultural aspects of both Southern Rhodesia and Zimbabwe in the preceding chapter, this chapter explores the educational implications of the coloniser's language policies in light of the Critical Language Planning (CLP) theory. As highlighted already, apart from undertaking this exercise to examine the impact of Rhodesian linguistic imperialism on this important sector of the society, efforts are also being made in the process to establish whether the Southern Rhodesian linguistic agenda is being maintained, advanced or eradicated. The background to this chapter is that education is an imperative 'resource' in facilitating development. The central role of education is to develop opportunities in lieu of constraints. Thus, education should strive to transform communities or the nation through human participation. Human participation is a 'symbol' interconnected with transformation. However, whilst education is the backbone of every modern society, not every form of it could yield proper progress towards the development of each and every community. This is so because development itself is relative such that whilst one form of it could prove to be quite perfect for one society it might prove to have flaws for another. This makes such an effort to focus on reviewing the effectiveness of the nature of education being offered quite pertinent to every country.

Defining Education

Education is the process of receiving or giving systematic instruction, especially at a school or university. It is a purposeful activity directed at achieving certain aims, such as transmitting knowledge or fostering skills and positive character traits. These aims may include the development of understanding, rationality, kindness and honesty. It is also pertinent to emphasise the importance of critical thinking in order to distinguish education from indoctrination. Education must, therefore, result in an improvement of the student as an individual and as a member of a particular community. This is the reason Gora and Mutasa (2015) assert that education should serve as a tool for immediate and continuous change in society. This is in line with the view that education stands for change, and this should be a positive change. Thus, apart from the maintenance of the acquired understanding of the environment, education must be able to turn the entire society into a more perfect home for everyone.

Educational Language Policy of Southern Rhodesia

Upon taking over control of the land between Zambezi and Limpopo rivers, the white settler government quickly resolved to respect the role of missionaries who had already initiated education of the locals with the motive of cultivating the necessary literacy for reading and spreading the gospel. The missionaries' ways were maintained, though efforts were made to ensure English (the new master's preferred language of imperialism) was to be introduced to the schools as a critical aspect of the curricula. This meant a slight deviation from the usual missionary approach to education that, instead, concentrated on instruction in indigenous languages and the reduction of these languages into writing for translation of the Bible. Their effort to cover every community saw them even going as far as introducing centres for teaching and translating the Bible using varieties of the same language such as Karanga, Zezuru, Korekore and Manyika. All this was due to their understanding of the effectiveness of education offered in the mother tongue.

Contrary to the missionary approach, the white settler government had other motives behind education. Whilst they were aware of the assured success of education delivered in the indigenous languages (as UNICEF asserted and encouraged), they tried to risk this effectiveness of the education by making sure teaching of almost every subject (including the indigenous languages themselves) was done in English. They never offered an opportunity for their translation into local languages as successfully done for the gospel by the missionaries. Rather, they denigrated the local languages as medieval and incapable of addressing 'complex issues' of modern society, thus adopting the evolutionist perception of dark races and the simplicity of their native languages. In light of the foregoing, a colonial educational reform was made, and a policy was introduced in which English became the official language for all native Zimbabweans, though they considered them very backward which would make mastering the 'complex language' (in the evolutionists' view) extremely difficult. So, in 1908 a committee on education, chaired by Hole, recommended that the educational system for Europeans, which was mostly voluntary, should be gradually replaced by a public school system financed by the state (Hungwe, 2007). It also recommended that the English language should be the sole medium of instruction in all schools serving the settlers (British South Africa Company (BSAC), 1908). In 1925, the Phelps-Stokes Commission on language policy went on to propose that 'the tribal' languages should be used in the lower elementary standards or grades to facilitate subsequent instruction in English.

The Commission's resolutions demonstrate the highest level of selfishness and disrespect there was for the locals and their languages. Gudhlanga (2005) notes that, in former Group B schools in high-density suburbs, Shona was only introduced as a subject in 1957 and Ndebele in 1967. In former Group A schools, Shona was only introduced in 1964; Zulu, instead of Ndebele, in 1977; and subsequently Ndebele in 1979. She adds that Shona found its way into the university in 1963 with Ndebele following in 1968. This proves how much the colonial government saw no need to rush the introduction of indigenous language education at a time they felt the need for their own language (English) to be honoured and used by foreigners as soon as possible. It pointed to the prevalence of some hidden agenda behind education during the colonial era.

As indicated already, indigenous languages were only accepted as media of instruction for the first three grades to prepare for English to take over from the fourth grade onwards. To ensure the supremacy of English and incentivise its learning across the country, at the same time placing the native English speakers (white settlers) at an unparalleled advantage in the country, proceeding to further studies required a pass in English, with Shona and Ndebele far from being considered alternatives (Gudhlanga, 2005). Thus, English served as the language of instruction and passing it as a subject became a must. This went the extra mile in enhancing the value of the English language together with its native speakers and their worldview at the expense of that of the local populace. It demonstrates how much the education got centred on the English language forcing every normal being to consider proficiency in English synonymous with a passport to a good life. All proper efforts were made to ensure its proper teaching as it had become the yardstick for one's success in education.

Contrary to the foregoing, Gudhlanga (2005) notes that even when Shona and Ndebele got introduced in schools, they were never taught by qualified personnel. This is in line with Chiwome (1996) who observed that, instead, their teachers were often chosen based on their spoken competence rather than professional training. Untrained white second-language learners often perceived themselves as competent enough to teach indigenous languages. In addition to that, the local languages had books on their grammar developed in English by English linguists such as George Fortune. The focus group discussants further highlighted how the indigenous languages were even taught in English, a condition local schools and most of the tertiary institutions are yet to reverse. They stressed how certain concepts in the indigenous languages' grammar, for instance, have always presented teachers with challenges when it comes to teaching them in the languages themselves. As if that was not enough, the learning slots allocated to these indigenous languages were quite unfavourable. The languages were normally taught in the hot afternoons when learners were tired with Mathematics, English, Science and other 'important' subjects permanently slotted for the fresh cool mornings demonstrating the lack of the coloniser's interest in the indigenous languages' proper teaching (Mhute, Mangeya, and Jakaza, 2021). Gudhlanga (2005) notes how in some schools these indigenous languages were just considered options to French or Latin (the so-called modern languages) and students often opted for the latter due to their love for adventure. This indicates how the locals were considered not so important that they were given an opportunity to either learn about themselves or other faraway societies instead. It is a clear testimony of how the centre got completely distanced from the locals through education, a condition this book considers the highest robbery the indigenous people have ever experienced.

To cement colonial hegemony, the white settler regime in 1970 forced Christian denominations to give up control of all schools and surrender them to the colonial government (Hungwe, 2007). This was the testimony of the colonial government's enhanced desire to considerably heighten control over all schools as it could no longer trust the church as its overseer of educational imperialism, especially due to an increase in nationalistic efforts to bring about emancipation from colonial rule. It confirmed how the promotion of the English language in education as well as naturalising the low status of the local ones was believed to ensure locals' desire to be white rather than see the presence of the imperialist as a threat. The colonial government made this drastic step even if it did not have a policy of teacher training as well as curriculum development to support minority languages (Ndlovu, 2015). Apart from explaining the marginalisation of minority languages in colonial education, it also points to a lack of respect for the indigenous languages as their suppression together with the local culture was part of their agenda.

Whilst traditional education on indigenous cultural issues was always done by well-experienced elders, education in all sectors was now attained in schools. Attending school became the norm for almost every child in no time replacing the traditional way considerably. This signalled the placement of English cultural aspects at the centre of locals' lives through education. Its mastery was made the only prerequisite to good life within the new society. That is why Gudhlanga (2005) notes that the syllabi were designed to portray the settler's culture as the epitome of civilisation in the then Southern Rhodesia, and the English language was presented as prestigious and the only gateway to success. Thus, education became an instrument for suppressing the local languages and the cultures they carried. To intensify this project of cultural segregation after 1965 when the anti-colonial opposition grew stronger, one new venture of the Rhodesian Front government was to launch the three-language African Times journal which was distributed freely to compete with the nationalist organisations for the support of the local populations in townships and Tribal Trust Lands. The journal exposed its readers to a regular bombardment with images of 'traditional' living and tales of harmonious co-operation between the white government and loyal chiefs.

Effects of Southern Rhodesian Educational Language Policy

The promotion of English and the relegation of local languages to the periphery in the colonial education set-up had far-reaching effects. The colonial regime readily introduced more serious Western education offered in English. It tied the two together sparking the impression that no other language could perfectly perform the task, a belief many people still hold over four decades into independence. The focus group discussants confirmed this belief throughout the country further highlighting its responsibility for the inability of efforts to empower indigenous languages in education. Chivhanga and Chimhenga (2013) rightly capture the situation by noting how in Southern Rhodesia the colonialists legislated the English language as the only capable medium of instruction in schools. Atkinson (1972) reiterates the idea by arguing that the chain reaction leading to the subsequent dominance of English in the school curriculum was set off in 1903 following the first education ordinance. He observes how, through a subtle tutelage, Africans in Zimbabwe came to regard English, and indeed associate it with knowledge, goodness, sweetness and an array of other positives. Those who could speak it received commendation and were made to feel that they were far better than those who could not speak it. For most Africans, English became synonymous with knowledge and education. Speaking good English was (wrongly of course) seen as an indicator that one was educated. English was, thus, associated with a good life, and as such, attitudes towards it became favourable. This was confirmed by the focus group discussants who noted that those unable to speak English were regarded as backward and useless.

English supremacy came at the expense of the many indigenous languages. Denial of an opportunity to use them for instruction, in a society where they are the most appropriate for promoting understanding, confirmed the sacredness of English as a mode of instruction to the locals. The delay in introducing them to school curricular asserted their uselessness together with the cultures they carried in the eyes of the locals. Placing them in the same bracket with languages like Portuguese spoken in places with nothing to do with their society further confirmed that. This promoted the white settler ideology of perceiving the multiplicity of the local languages as a liability rather than an asset. The arrangement justified the need to learn aspects like foreign histories and geographies instead of local ones using foreign lenses. In other words, it worked well for the colonial administration by preparing the locals for acceptance of foreign stuff, thereby eradicating the possibilities of questions on the absence of local ones and the presence of the English as the administrators of the country. This shows how the language of instruction cemented the imperialist's idea of transferring the centre from Southern Rhodesia to regions that are thousands of miles away.

Speakers of the minoritised languages found themselves robbed the most by the 1931 arrangement. Apart from having to compulsorily learn English as a second language, they found themselves bound to learn a third language as a national language. This meant the arrangement obliged them to become trilingual. In school, their children were the most disadvantaged as their learning was to be in the second and third languages. This automatically placed them way behind the rest as competing with first- and second-language speakers is always quite difficult. In this regard, the informants brought to light the fact that many parents tried their level best to lessen their children's burden by making them acquire the national language involved and learn English as a second language. In most cases, due to their environment, the children ended up having to simultaneously acquire the minority language and the national language, at times with subtractive bilingualism negatively impacting the life of the minority language.

The whole education system that overemphasised the importance of foreign languages and lifestyles served the white man well as it made a permanent mark on the nation. It generated workers bent on loyally serving the white master. Another good example is the approach to key societal aspects like politics. Even if waves from other countries opposed to colonialism later supported the ideas of a revolution, the educational system gave rise to Western-oriented leaders who believed in nothing other than the emulation of the former coloniser's administration. This saw power being transferred at independence to a leadership with no desire and ability to completely transform the system of governance from the inherited one, a move that ensured the country remained a proper home for the white settlers. A good example is the respect still commanded by English in Zimbabwean administrative issues. The judiciary, for instance, is still guided along Western ways and writings. The same applies to economics, health and all other vital sectors of society. In short, one can argue that the settler education laid a firm foundation for the continuation of the Western political, economic and sociocultural ways by vitalising English ways through its media of instruction.

Zimbabwean Educational Language Policy

To demonstrate the impact of the neglect of indigenous languages in education, one can refer to the policy adopted after independence which did not bring considerable changes to the educational language policy. Upon attainment of political independence in 1980, Zimbabwe transformed the education system into patches and shreds possibly because changing the whole curriculum was an expensive undertaking. Based on the recommendation of the Nziramasanga Commission of 1999 and the Narrative Report of 2014, Zimbabwean education was later completely overhauled, as reflected in the new 2015–2022 curriculum framework (MoPSE, 2015), in answer to deficits noted in the socio-economic spheres. The reform process was then an opportunity to make changes that could possibly resonate with the wishes and aspirations of Zimbabweans.

Prior to the new reforms of 2015, Zimbabwe made several strides in the language policy in schools. From 1980 to 1987, English was the sole language examined in Grade 7. Seven years after independence, the Zimbabwe government passed the Education Act of 1987 to address the dominance and hegemony of English in particular and the transformation of the colonial language policy in general (Sibanda, 2019). The Education Act of 1987 was notable for articulating the following provisions for educational language policy:

1. The three main languages of Zimbabwe, namely, Shona, Ndebele, and English, shall be taught in all primary schools from the first grade as follows:
   a. Shona and English in all areas where the mother tongue of the majority or the residences is Shona, or
   b. Ndebele and English in all areas where the mother tongue of the majority or the residence is Ndebele.
2. Prior to the fourth grade, either Shona or Ndebele may be used as the medium of instruction depending upon which language is more commonly spoken and better understood by pupils.
3. From the fourth grade, English shall be the medium of instruction provided that Shona or Ndebele shall be taught as subjects on equal time allocation as the English language.
4. In areas where minority languages exist, the minister may authorise the teaching of such languages in primary schools (Government of Zimbabwe, 1987).

It also recognised six minority languages for use as languages of initial instruction as well, namely, Tonga, Kalanga, Nambya, Venda, Shangani and Sotho. I must also emphasise that whilst stern efforts were made in the right direction in the 1980s to make Shona and Ndebele pre-requisites in teacher training, this was unfortunately abolished in the late 1980s.

Further revision of the policy was made in 1990. It brought about the introduction of Shona and Ndebele as examination subjects in Grade 7, exactly ten years after the attainment of national independence. However, apart from this achievement, it showed considerable weaknesses, as observed by Shizha (2012), that it re-enforced the dominance and hegemony of English and strengthened the earlier transitional model aimed at a single target language (English) at the end of the school pipeline. Furtherance to this, whilst revision of the Education Act in 2006 allowed instruction in minor indigenous languages such as Tonga and Kalanga and permitted the teaching of Shona, Ndebele and English, these changes were merely on paper and not in practice.

Similarly, the Constitution of Zimbabwe Amendment (No.20) Act of 2013 is perceived as a model of linguistic democracy in terms of its recognition of 16 languages, 15 of which are indigenous, yet no notable efforts are done towards ensuring their teaching and use as media of instruction in the areas they are spoken. The Education Amendment Act (No.15), 2020 advances that every school shall endeavour to:

(a) Teach every officially recognised language;
(b) Ensure that the language of instruction shall be the language of examination;
(c) Ensure that the mother tongue is to be used as a medium of instruction in early childhood education.

Some colleges of teacher education in Zimbabwe continue to offer the two local languages to trainee teachers, leaving all the other thirteen unattended to, despite the call for all learner teachers to be competent in at least three local languages. Gora and Mutasa (2015) note that it is important to note that the teaching of some of the minoritised languages is also underway from Grades 1 to 7. Examining of Tonga at the Grade 7 level began in 2011, whilst that of Venda, Nambya and Kalanga started in 2012, and that of Xichangana was pencilled for 2013 (Dube, 2012). However, they are quick to observe that preparations to have the languages taught and examined at the secondary school level are at a very slow pace although the syllabi have been availed to schools. Similarly, just like what was experienced for Shona and Ndebele during the colonial era, there is a lack of qualified personnel to teach these other indigenous languages at secondary schools. This was captured by Gora, Mavhunga, Muringai and Waniwa (2010) who say what disturbs is the fact that in most instances the teachers assigned to teach Tonga language as a subject in primary schools are not qualified to do so. This is so in spite of the fact that in the late 1990s some teacher training colleges were entrusted with the responsibility of training personnel for teaching these minority languages. It is also worrisome that no efforts are in place to use local languages in teaching other subject areas like what is happening with English demonstrating that in practice it is way above all the other languages. No concrete will is also visible in Zimbabwean universities to promote the use and teaching of the languages too. Only a few, like Great Zimbabwe University (whose niche hinges on cultural heritage), are making efforts to do so by offering the languages entirely in minority languages.

Effects of the Zimbabwean Educational Language Policy

Zimbabwean education still shows evidence of advancing the objectives and tone set by the colonial regime. This is in line with Shizha and Kariwo (2011) who enunciate that colonial education policymakers defined the education system that they deemed necessary for Africans and planned and administered it according to their political and economic agendas. It is still evident decades after independence that in designing the school curriculum, the colonial policymakers did not make any effort to design an education system that harmonised the needs of different racial and ethnic groups in Zimbabwe. The Zimbabwean education system is struggling to provide equal opportunities to all indigenous languages. In this regard, Nhongo (2013), Sibanda (2019) and Shizha (2012) note how various surveys show that educationists, researchers, observers and policy analysts are alarmed and disappointed by continuities rather than a transformation in the language policy introduced after independence in Zimbabwe.

The fact that tertiary institutions in Zimbabwe extol English language as the language for intelligence, participation and development (by saying for one to be offered a programme of study in their chosen career path at a local university or college, their academic qualifications should include English language) has immensely affected people's perception of English in education. The same is evident at the secondary level as well where for a learner to proceed to the advanced level their ordinary level certificate should include a pass in English language and other four subjects. Instead of discarding the legacy of English by creating a learning model framework that accommodates all officially recognised indigenous languages by ensuring that English language is not exclusively prioritised as a subject or language point of entry or graduation to a higher stage within the education circles, the nation is showing no real interest in promoting the role of indigenous languages. The multiplicity of languages continues to be perceived as a burden in line with the former imperial power's preferred ideology. The book agrees with Gora and Mutasa's (2015) observation that whilst many scholars may argue that, in the face of globalisation and modernisation, the study of indigenous languages no longer matters much, there is a great need for such specialisation for the development and management of human resources that draw from these languages. It regards most of the challenges negatively impacting the effectiveness of the Zimbabwean education system as a result of the unfair diglossic landscape created and still nourished by linguistic imperialism decades into independence.

In education, the focus group discussants indicated that the impact of linguistic imperialism is immense. They noted with great concern how much parents wish to have their children instructed in English at the expense of their own first languages. In spite of the economic hardships being faced, many parents ensure at all costs that their children make it to very expensive 'English-only' schools. Such parents, as alluded to already, even go to the extent of hiring considerably expensive maids with passes in ordinary level English in a bid to maximise exposure of their children to the English language at the expense of the indigenous languages. Nyaungwa (2013) notes that the alienation brought about by the continued use of English (a foreign language) as the official language is so entrenched that many indigenous Zimbabweans have come to accept it unconsciously. It is evident that most Zimbabweans have come to think and accept that English is superior to all the indigenous languages. The knowledge that one language leads to advancement and success in life and an awareness that the knowledge of an indigenous language is not enough to lead one anywhere in terms of material success has greatly reinforced this mindset. In such a situation, it is, therefore, not uncommon to find many parents striving to send their children to former white-only schools where they are assured of enhanced support for the learning of English. Other informants further observed that nowadays most parents' desire to send their children to a school depends on the school's performance in the English language. This explains why almost every parent takes more pride in a child's pass or better performance in the English language at school. One interviewee scoffed at how, upon being told about a child's collection of examination results, the parents quickly asked about their symbol for the English language. It demonstrates how much the entire nation has come to accept that the norm is for everyone to excel in the former coloniser's language more than four decades after independence.

Since parents are the first models for their children, the perception of English as superior and the only gateway to success has become deeply engrained in the children too. This is in line with Magwa's (2015) finding that, just like the learners, the teachers, and lecturers too, prefer English to be used as a medium of instruction in education. In his survey, a total of 135 (67.5%) teachers and lecturers indicated on a questionnaire that they would prefer English as opposed to Shona or Ndebele to be the sole medium of instruction in education. A similar pattern also emerged from the interviews he conducted where both learners and their teachers preferred English instead of the use of any African language as the medium of instruction. According to Magwa's study, it was 60% of teachers/lecturers and 70% of learners who indicated during the interviews that they would want to use English as the official medium of instruction, and parents too expressed attitudes similar to those of learners, teachers and lecturers. The reason they said this, as confirmed by the current focus group discussion, is because they perceive English as associated with power, prestige and success. They are not even bothered by the advantage the mother languages would bring to their understanding of the learned concepts. This situation is captured by Kamwendo (1999, p. 229) who says, 'English is synonymous with the sound education whilst education through African languages is given second class rating'. Some people have even started perceiving it as an easier medium for expressing their perceptions when compared to their mother tongues. This certifies the idea that the alienation resulting from linguistic imperialism has gone too far that the local people are even looking forward to dreaming and even crying in the former coloniser's language. This is a clear indication of the extent to which the Southern Rhodesian linguistic imperialism agenda has successfully cultivated admiration for the former coloniser as well as self-hate within the locals. It is in line with Adegbija's (1994, p. 104) argument that 'provision of education in the vernacular rather than an international language (like English) arouses resentment among students and parents'.

It is critical to stress that by destroying the country's belief in the power vested in indigenous languages, linguistic imperialism has cemented Zimbabwe's position as a developing nation as education could hardly inspire proper progress towards development. This is in line with Mazrui's (2009) argument that no country has ever developed using a foreign language and Mhute's (2014) assertion that only instruction in a first language can guarantee effective learning that facilitates creativity with the acquired educational concepts. It explains the inability of locally produced graduates like technicians, engineers and doctors to come up with befitting solutions for local challenges, a move that has recently seen them looking to other continents for all solutions for their own challenges like local coronavirus variants. The position is also shared by Tackie-Ofosu, Mahama, Vandyck, Dosoo, Kumador and Toku (2015) whose survey results indicated that both parents and teachers appreciate the importance of the mother tongue, with reasons including its power to promote cultural identity, easy understanding of educational concepts and for effective communication. Thus, the use of the mother tongue in education ensures excellent comprehension of concepts and ideas. Unfortunately, evidence of the disappearance of faith in indigenous languages is provided by Magwa's (2015) observation that the few parents (30%) who preferred the use of an African language as the medium of instruction were quick to say that this was the situation in all the developed countries. In this regard, I am arguing that the reason Africa is bedevilled by so many challenges for decades after independence is because of the replacement of its traditional ways with an education that, due to its mode of instruction, fails to be as effective as it is to its originators. Whilst the same education is allowing the former colonisers opportunities to make commendable developmental strides, it is only making most Africans poorer, hopeless and more dependent. This is the reason Moto (2002, p. 43) argues that 'if Africans are to attain realistic developmental and economical value, there has to be a well thought out and carefully articulated policy on media of instruction'. The position is reiterated by Ndlovu and Du Plessis (2018, p. 1) who comment that the exclusive use of former colonial languages and dominant African languages in education in Africa is an obstacle to achieving access to quality education for ethnic minority language speakers.

In the light of all that has been said, it is safe to assert that Zimbabwean education has remained completely colonised through the media of instruction. Due to the media of instruction, the goal of education has remained distanced from us, yet the education is modelled and delivered by us to ourselves. In other words, instead of understanding that learning is all about being enlightened about our nature in order to make the best out of our own surroundings, we tend to think of knowing more of those away from us for their approval.

We are always learning with the emulation of the so-called developed nations (especially the English speakers) in mind. Such an approach would never make us equal to or better than them. This is why Teasley and Butler (2020) argue that the global project of decolonising education must begin with epistemic justice that de-centres Eurocentric hegemonic power relationships by valuing the knowledge production of racialised and indigenous others in areas related to institutional cultures, curricula and pedagogic practices. In this regard, the replacement of English with indigenous languages as media of instruction in Zimbabwe is the main step and the logical point of departure towards real decolonisation of education. The chapter argues that, through the medium of instruction, this education inherited from the coloniser has refused to let go of the flavour meant to characterise it by its originator. Revisiting this medium would obviously avail the long overdue slight twist in the education's focus whose absence has made it inadequate as far as our empowerment is concerned to this date.

Unfortunately, the sacredness of the medium of instruction does not seem to significantly fade from our minds. For instance, tertiary institutions in Zimbabwe extol English language as the language for intelligence, participation and development. For instance, for one to be offered a programme of study in their chosen career path at a local university or college, their academic qualifications should include English language. The same is evident at the secondary level as well where, for a learner to proceed to 'A' level, their 'O' level certificate should include a pass in English language and other four subjects. This is the reason Gora and Mutasa (2015) note that being competent in English has been equated to being educated, and it has become the highest of the people's source of pride. It is critical to note as well that all this happened to the detriment of the indigenous languages. In this regard, it is hereby argued that the proper development of indigenous languages will never take place unless the English language legacy is seriously wiped out of the Zimbabwean educational framework. There is need to create a learning model framework that accommodates all officially recognised indigenous languages. Efforts have to be made to reverse the current situation where English language is the only prioritised mode of instruction, language subject and language point of entry for graduation to tertiary education. Hence Batibo's (2015, p. 16) argument that 'to ensure a holistic development, language should be involved at all levels, from infancy to adulthood'. Wolff (2016, p. 1) reiterates the position by asserting that 'development is based on communication through language... and language becomes a highly relevant factor in all sectors of political, social, cultural and economic life'. In the light of the foregoing, there is need for Zimbabwean legislators to rethink the reason language is considered a human right in order to understand the colonial goal behind making English the sole medium of instruction in the education of native speakers of other languages.

It is critical to highlight that as long as there is no recognition of local languages, education would not enlighten the Zimbabwean population as much as it could. The informants for this study asserted sternly that the source of our nation's problems is the failure in education. Whilst currently Zimbabwe is prominent for its competence in the English language within the entire continent, she is equally infamous for aspects like poor governance, poverty, corruption, starvation, unemployment and calls for various forms of aid. If ensuring excellency in English meant the effectiveness of education, then proper interventions in the challenges listed above would have been assured. This only proves the ineffectiveness of the education programme, and Nyaungwa (2013) supports this by arguing that the use of English as a language of instruction in education hinders more than facilitates children's learning which is the reason a cursory look at districts' statistics tend to reveal that many secondary schools usually score higher passes in Shona and Ndebele than in other subject areas instructed in English. This has remained the case even at a time learners often go for extra lessons for these subjects taught in English and rarely do so for the indigenous languages.

The Zimbabwean educational products, as observed by Mhute and Musingafi (2015), have no capacity to be creative with the educational concepts for the generation of solutions for the problems at hand. This chapter argues that education must be for the generation of solutions for problems at hand and the inability to do so proves that the national education system is in urgent need of a serious visit. Amongst the main aspects, it requires a reconsideration of the language of instruction to replace it with one that ensures the most appropriate instruction for the local populace. If this is not done, the nation would continue trailing in developmental issues. The chapter, thus, agrees with Gora and Mutasa (2015) who argue that despite some curriculum reforms after the attainment of independence, the effects of colonial language policy and language planning with regard to the Zimbabwean education system seem to have remained intact. It is still advancing the belief that English assures us of the best possible life today and in the future whereas in actual fact it intends to keep us dependent which is typical of colonial education.

To stress the impact linguistic imperialism has had on locals, an informant alluded to efforts that are being made to fight against any traces of other indigenous languages. To illustrate this, she shared an article in the *Newzimbabwe* on 19 October 2022 reporting on Silobela community rejecting qualified non-Ndebele-speaking teachers on the pretext of protecting their language and culture as evident in the image Figure 6.1.

This clearly demonstrates how the colonial language policy-based division still stands in Zimbabwe over four decades after independence. No one has ever dared to question the clear effects of English as the sole media of instruction on their languages and cultures to this date. Instead, every corner of the country takes pride in the deployment of native English language speakers to their areas but cannot accommodate speakers of a fellow indigenous language

Figure 6.1

who share most of the cultural norms and values with them. We can hardly tolerate our own fellow Zimbabweans yet comfortable with foreign nationals sharing very little, if any, with us which clarifies the impact of linguistic imperialism on our nation.

Conclusion

The chapter has demonstrated that education in a foreign language is a major tool the imperialists employed in order to tame the mindset of their colony even after independence. They considered education a very powerful tool for inculcating their target perceptions of life and their entire environment. In other words, education was properly positioned to reorient the colony and make it properly understand and become the so-called modern and civilised society that the imperial power wants it to become. The subjects and curricula that were introduced went a great way in ensuring this order become a reality. This is the reason, during and after colonisation, in Zimbabwe the history and geography the education got preoccupied with is mainly centred on the regions foreign to our own. West African history and the geographic aspects of Europe and America are still being vitalised.

The chapter demonstrates how the English language has been made a key focus in Zimbabwean education and efforts are being made to portray it as an indispensable feature of proper education forever. The curricula covertly prescribe English as the sole perfect language that can be studied and used for instruction in the Zimbabwean classroom (Gora, 2014). Over 40 years after independence, there is still a perception of the success of the education exercise as determined by one's mastery of the English language. As a subject, failing to pass it makes a certificate inadequate for consideration for higher education or employment. Thus, in line with the evolutionist perspective, the belief in local languages as backward, simplistic and incapable of handling aspects of the so-called sophisticated realities of advanced societies was ingrained into the Zimbabwean community. This explains the efforts that have been made to this date to see the position of English in the national language configuration maintained. Efforts are always in place to promote its role as the language of instruction and many minds within the country are quite convinced that no local language could serve as an equal or better mode for the successful teaching of science subjects. This is in spite of the fact that other countries are doing so successfully in and out of the African continent.

The chapter argued that the use of English as an indispensable subject and language of instruction has resulted in indigenous languages being thrown to the periphery in the education set-up. They have been relegated to useless codes that are good for nothing as demonstrated by their learning being made optional in some cases with people able to go for the so-called modern languages like French, Germany, Portuguese and Italian. At some point, the University of Zimbabwe (the then sole university in the country) even went as far as dedicating an entire department to them (Department of Modern Languages) at a time more than 15 of the indigenous languages were not even being considered for teaching at the institution. This is perceived as a clear testimony of the breakthrough of linguistic imperialism in the educational sector. It is further confirmed by the fact that no proper consideration of teaching of most of the languages recognised by the 2013 constitution has been done nine years after the recommendation. In that regard, the chapter ends by highlighting the fact that such a position is the most effective recipe for a nation's educational failure. It alludes to the need for proper emancipation of education from the clutches of linguistic imperialism if education is to become effective and empowering to the local communities. Without this, education remains a tool for advancing the imperialist's political, economic and sociocultural agenda in the country.

7 Conclusion and Way Forward

Introduction

The preceding chapters have clearly demonstrated the central role linguistic imperialism plays in nourishing all the other forms of imperialism. It has been proven to be the blood running in the veins of the entire colonial set-up. The chapters further demonstrated how much harm the maintenance of the colonial language policy is doing to the various sectors of Zimbabwe by sustaining coloniality. The thesis of the current chapter is to present some concluding remarks as well as suggest the possible way forward for Zimbabwe and postcolonies in a similar situation.

Conclusion

The situation transpiring in Zimbabwe has been proven to be confirming the Critical Language Planning theory's argument that language is, in actual fact, a force that determines how communities are administered politically, economically, socioculturally and educationally. Politically, it is clear that the belief and desire for English, which stems from linguistic imperialism, has strongly tied the nation to foreign political policies, especially those linked to the English-speaking former coloniser some of which are proving very inappropriate. The same is also true of the impact that the effort to marginalise indigenous languages for English's benefit has partitioned the country into Shona speaking and Ndebele speaking. The friction between the two sides has seriously compromised unity within the country leading to serious misunderstandings such as the Gukurahundi conflict from 1982 to 1986/7 whose effects are still visible within the country. Resolution efforts like the Unity Accord between ZANU PF's Robert Gabriel Mugabe and Joshua Nkomo (both late) have cemented the distinction so much that political parties make efforts to make sure leadership is composed of Shona speakers with a Ndebele second vice president. The book argues that such endeavours are quite compromising to all progressive people's desire to solely focus on capability when electing their leaders. The impact is also heightened by the fact that the resultant singling out of the speakers of these two languages facilitated a permanent political marginalisation of all the other indigenous languages. Consequently, to this date, no efforts are even made to seriously consider the possibility of having an able president from them. Thus, whilst it appears like just marginalisation of the languages in day-to-day use, their speakers have been fully relegated to non-entities in political circles together with them. This affects their participation in all political systems as well, and the book argues that such a situation is both anti-democratic and not progressive. It even defeats the 'Second Republic's *Nyika inovakwa nevene vayo*' (A nation is built by its owners) mantra as it relegates a considerable fraction of the people belonging to this group of owners to the periphery when the capable ones are not known yet. The set-up breeds a lot of effort as well to sabotage developmental political efforts that could be put in place as the minoritised language speakers have always demonstrated dissatisfaction with the priorities being given to Shona and Ndebele at their expense.

Whilst Zimbabwe, like many other post-colonies, readily consider English and other languages left behind by the colonial era neutral language options which unity within the country could be ensured, it has been demonstrated that harmony is being ensured through keeping the Shona and Ndebele groups away from each other instead of an arrangement that effectively bind all locals together as members of the same nation. This is the reason conflicts readily erupt between the two groups whenever a chance crops up, like what transpired during premier league soccer matches involving sides from these two major languages in the country. A good example is the 2001 incident that saw Highlanders FC (mainly Ndebele speaking), Dynamos FC and Masvingo United FC (both mainly Shona speaking) being punished following a wave of violence. Highlanders and Masvingo United fans were involved in serious clashes that left one fan dead, several others injured and property worth thousands of dollars damaged in the last league match of the 2000 season on 19 November in Masvingo's Mucheke Stadium (Kariati, 2001). The same applies to speakers of the other languages that felt heavily minoritised by being bunched under Shona and Ndebele in 1931. The research established that the move generated some bitterness for the two indigenous languages they were bunched into (like the one between Kalanga speakers and Ndebeles) and such an environment has been considered politically unhealthy for the country. It has been argued that whereas the country, just like many other post colonies, is quick to brush aside the effort for replacing English as a lingua franca in practice, the move does not fully unite the nation.

In the same way as the political sector, economically, foreign policies have remained key to the country as well. Dependence on a foreign language has ushered in foreign economic approaches, some of which have even backfired heavily causing a lot of damage to the country, for instance, the Economic Structural Adjustment Programme (ESAP), an International Monetary Fund and World Bank-inspired policy of the 1990s which fuelled inflation and unemployment that the country is still battling more than three decades after.

Worth noting as well is the dependence on foreign aiding institutions like the World Bank and International Monetary Fund that has remained at the heart of the independent country. Of late this has led to the cries that have come to be typical of the nation due to resolutions to deny her further assistance following her failure to settle her long overdue debts. This dependence syndrome resulting from the unnecessary dependence on English and its economic lifestyle has also been fuelling efforts to link up with the East for want of a replacement for the usual reliance on the Western societies, especially the former imperial power, Britain. The move has since led to considerable exploitation, for instance, in the form of mining deals whose benefit to the country has since been questioned by many people.

The book has also emphasised that along with ignoring indigenous languages, the country is also making the mistake of ignoring prospective local solutions to her economic problems. It demonstrates that whilst developed countries found their breakthroughs from local solutions blended with Western ways, like China's traditional herbs and Japan's traditional rice, Zimbabwean focus is entirely foreign which has allowed ignorance of the indigenous knowledge systems capable of making a difference. This has failed the country considerably resulting in record inflation, unemployment and poverty, amongst others. It, thus, confirms Phillipson's (1992) argument that linguistic imperialism takes place within an overarching structure of asymmetrical North/South relations, where language interlocks with other dimensions like culture (particularly in education, science and the media), economy and politics.

Socioculturally, the book has stressed the link between language and culture by demonstrating how much linguistic imperialism impacts on sociocultural aspects of society. It shows the extent to which the nation has come to believe in English or foreign ways in areas like religion, health and philosophy. This is having dire effects on the country, for instance, the replacement of the *Unhu/ Vumunhu/Ubuntu* philosophy with an individualistic one (ushered in by the promotion of a foreign language and its lifestyle) has led to practices like corruption as well as too much greedy for materialistic things leading to practices like child abuse and human trafficking for monetary benefits. The book lays bare the fact that upholding the diktats of linguistic imperialism is negatively impacting the attitude of the nation towards the local sociocultural practices as the people are going too far as far as eradicating traces of their identity is concerned. This has seen people taking injections, creams and even powders to make themselves lighter in complexion, for example. There are also efforts to dye and lengthen hair with others putting on artificial braids and weaves just to appear like the native English people. This shows how far the people have gone due to self-hate and love for English and its lifestyle. Unfortunately, some of the efforts have resulted in critical side effects such as skin cancer the effects of which are further heightened by the unavailability of the necessary machinery locally to combat them.

The precious national heritage is also vanishing completely due to the increased delay in restoration of the indigenous languages and their cultures to their places. The area of indigenous knowledge systems has been emphasised in the book stressing the idea that many elders dying together with their priceless knowledge as many often fail to find youngsters who are prepared to be entrusted with it due to allegiance to foreign religions that castigate everything typical of the Zimbabwean tradition as medieval, evil and overdue for extinction. The area of traditional herbs (whose side effects the study established were extremely minimal) has been hit the hardest and the book sees no chances for regaining such invaluable asserts. The value of the loss has been proven to be invaluable considering how most countries developed through their own indigenous knowledge systems.

The area of education has been presented as also being negatively impacted by linguistic imperialism. The book demonstrates how, due to linguistic imperialism, the nation has come to consider it more advantageous to use English as a medium of instruction than using indigenous languages. The perception gets support from Mutasa (2004, p. 121) who says 'the world can survive without South Africa, but South Africa cannot exist without the world'. Thus, they perceive the use of English as properly positioning educational products for perfectly fitting into the global community. This book, however, considers this perception to negatively impact the success of the educational exercise. The perception is shared by Mchazime (1999, p. 41) who argues that the first language helps the child to establish both emotional and intellectual closeness with his or her parents. Since most parents communicate their feelings in their own language, they are also able to transmit aspects of their culture to the child in that language. It makes learning in such a language easier and more effective as it is the one in which the child's surrounding environment is defined. This is in line with the Sapir-Whorf hypothesis which asserts that we think in our mother tongue, which makes learning in a local language more effective, and the reason developed countries always have their students taught in indigenous languages.

Whilst Zimbabwean education is internationally ranked considerably high, the book stresses the inability of educational products to bring about real solutions for local problems like poverty (even when Zimbabwe has much more wealth than many developed countries, for instance, in terms of mineral deposits), unemployment and the sky-rocketing inflation. This is considered a sign of the ineffectiveness of the education process with the reason being mainly the language of instruction. This is why most of the best graduates in the country think of nothing other than securing employment in foreign lands whilst in developed countries they generate jobs for many people. This points to some missing link in the quality of education our graduates have attained as it does not fully empower them to control their destiny through mastering their own environment in the same way it does for those in developed countries. This proves that the focus of local education is still bent on generating employees rather than employers, an approach that was meant to sustain the colonial set-up when the white settlers were meant to be the sole masters.

Possible Way Forward

The book suggests that we come to an understanding that the duty of the coloniser was, above everything else, to disorient the local populace in order to generate the kind of subject they so desired. There is need to understand the importance of a mother tongue from the fact that, even if the white settlers were very few on setting foot in the country, they could not opt to learn any one language spoken by the locals for communication purposes but rather forced the many local people to learn their own native language for official communication. It is also critical to note that whilst the country attained political emancipation in 1980, the blood of political imperialism still runs in nation's veins in the form of linguistic imperialism. We must, therefore, see the true function of linguistic imperialism during our time, which is keeping the fire of colonialism burning in our country and the reason the former coloniser, through the British Council, is eager to always invest in the maintenance of English libraries across the nation. This set-up obliges us to constantly depend on foreigners for funding and other critical forms of assistance and even try to hold the former imperial power responsible for all our troubles despite our bragging about our nation being 'a sovereign state that will never be a colony again', thus in the words of the late former president, Robert Gabriel Mugabe.

Politically, it is high time the nation starts realising the exact manner in which English ensures some unity and peace in the country. It does not eradicate the enmity between us as members of the country but rather makes us ignore the hatred within members of the different indigenous languages. However, this only suffices as long as there are no sparks for quarrelling. We must, therefore, invest in our own indigenous lingua franca that we are all happy to identify with in the same way Swahili is in Tanzania and other East African countries or Mandarin Chinese in China. This way we would boost the perception of the entire populace as one and consider building our country to be our own duty, as captured by the second republic's *'Nyika inovakwa nevene vayo'* (a nation is built by its owners) mantra.

We have to reposition our centre and desist from thinking about the global picture as the nation's primary concern (an approach that was typical of and appropriate for the foreign white settlers who intended to make sure their own home country remain the centre for all British territories). This way we would think of fitting and surviving comfortably within our own environment before the global village. To do this we must think of understanding ourselves fully before burdening ourselves (in terms of nature, troubles and opportunities) with understanding foreign societies. We must think of generating local solutions to our own problems rather than concentrating on begging the international community for intervention in every situation (an approach strategically implanted by the coloniser for colonies to always perceive themselves as dependents). We would think of local answers to our questions rather than continuously depending on external researchers, a position that would make us believe in ourselves. This way we would not bother ourselves with foreign approval for things good for our own community. It would ultimately translate to real independence for our nation and one way of ensuring this is by prioritising local languages more than foreign ones.

Our society must develop an understanding of the importance of its own identity. Positive development focuses on improving what is there rather than completely replacing everything. We have to realise that all developed countries maintain the roles of their philosophies, beliefs, languages, norms and values at the centre of their societies. We, therefore, need to realise that the former imperial power tricked us into believing that all that is typical of us is medieval, evil and due for extinction. It is, therefore, time to note that, without reversing this mentality, we would never find our ground and remain dependent forever. This calls for an immediate reinstatement of our philosophies, belief systems, languages, norms and values (of course with the necessary externally inspired modifications where necessary) before their traces vanish forever. The current education's new curriculum's emphasis on the reinstatement of *Unhu/ Vumunhu/ Ubuntu* philosophy and the various lessons on traditional cultures is a step in the right direction but one that must not be an end in itself. Efforts must be put in place to go beyond just learning about them to modifying our daily practices along those lines.

There is need to understand that proper education focuses on bringing about an enhanced understanding of the environment. The focus starts from the immediate environment going out. This means we must first understand ourselves before we endeavour to know more about those away from us. It is critical to know that we can understand ourselves better when taught in the language in which we received our orientation upon being introduced into this world for the first time. This means we must reinstate our own indigenous languages as the media of instruction if education is to yield the best possible results. It is pertinent as well to learn from the missionaries who (before the coloniser) had to emphasise the offering of education in indigenous languages. This was because they realised that reaching the souls of the people required real understanding which is only attainable in one's mother tongue. They also managed to do this as they had no hidden motives and the reason the coloniser, due to the focus on exploitation, could not withstand this kind of education resulting in the instatement of English as the face of the learning process.

Our government must take advantage of the 2013 constitution's position on languages and start implementing it in all sectors. It must rekindle the long-lost people's attitudes towards their own identities. This calls for policies that push the various societies towards their own traditional practices, a move that would lobby for them to not only maintain the invaluable traditional systems but also reconstruct those that are vanishing. This could be done, for instance, by incentivising the efforts through competitions and rewards. This is only possible after the governing body understands the essence of the heritages to national survival and development.

Finally, it remains critical to understand that language is far from being a mere code of communication. It is, in fact, a force that determines who we are, how we understand each other and how we understand and relate to others. We must learn from developed countries on how we must treat our own languages. Decisions on them must also be made by us for us rather than by a selfish exploiter for us.

References

Acemoglu, D. S. J., & Robinson, J. A. (2005). The rise of Europe: Atlantic trade, institutional change, and economic growth. *American Economic Review, 95*(3), 546–579.

Adegbija, E. (1994). *Language attitudes in sub-saharan Africa: A sociolinguistic overview.* Clevedon: Multilingual Matters Ltd.

Adelman, C., Kemmis, S., & Jenkins, D. (1980). Rethinking case study: Notes from the second Cambridge Conference. In H. Simons (Ed.), *Towards a science of the singular* (pp. 45–61). Centre for Applied Research in Education, University of East Anglia.

Adhikari, M. (2010). A total extinction confidently hoped for: The destruction of Cape San society under Dutch colonial rule, 1700–1795. *Journal of Genocide Research, 12*(1&2), 19–44.

Anderson, B. (1983). *Imagined communities: Reflections on the origin and spread of nationalism.* London: Sage.

Anyidoho, K. (1992). Language and development strategy in pan-African literary experience. *Research in African Literatures, 23,* 45–63.

Atkinson, N. D. (1972). The missionary contribution to early education in Rhodesia. In J. Anthony (Ed.), *Christianity south of the Zambezi* (Vol. 1, pp. 83–96). Salisbury: Mambo Press.

Beach, D. (1994). *A Zimbabwean past.* Gweru: Mambo Press.

Batibo, H. (2015). *Language decline and death in Africa: Causes, consequences and challenges.* Clevedon: Multilingual Matters.

Berg, B. L. (2001). *Qualitative research methods for the social sciences.* Needham Heights, MA: Allyn & Bacon.

Bhabha, H. (1984). *Of mimicry and man: Ambivalence of colonial discourse.* London: Sage.

Bharadvaja, M. (n.d.). *Theories and Mechanisms of Imperialism and Expansion of European Empires.* Ram Lal Anand College (Morning), New Delhi: University of Delhi.

Benett, G. (1962). *Concept of empire 1774–1947.* London: Sage.

Bostock, W. W. (2018). South Africa's evolving language policy: Educational implications. *Journal of Curriculum and Teaching, 7*(2), 38–50.

British South Africa Company (BSA). (1908). Rhodesia under company rule. In *The 1911 encyclopaedia Britannica.*

Broodryk, J. (2005). *Understanding South Africa: The Ubuntu way of living.* Pretoria: Ubuntu School of Philosophy.

References

Bunkachou. (2002). Korekara no Jidai ni Motomerareru Kokugoryoku. Retrieved August 3, 2020, from http://www.mext.go.jp/b_menu/shingi/toushin/04020301/003.htm.

Canhanga, M. V., & Banda M. (2017). Education language policy in Mozambique: A critical view. *International Journal of Humanities Social Sciences and Education (IJHSSE)*, 4(5), 12–21.

Chimhundu, H. (1993). The status of African languages in Zimbabwe. *Southern Africa Political and Economic Monthly*, 7(1), 57–59.

Chimhundu, H. (1999). The Agenda for African Languages Research Institute (ALRI). Paper presented to the ALEX Project International Seminar on the theme: Taking African languages into the New Millennium at the Organisational Training and Development Centre, Harare.

Chimhundu, H. (2002). *Final report: Language policies in Africa: Intergovernmental conference on language policies in Africa*. Harare: UNESCO.

Chiromo, A. (2006). *Research methods and statistics in education: A student's guide*. Gweru: Beta Print.

Chivhanga, E., & Chimhenga, S. (2013). Language planning. In Zimbabwe: The use of indigenous languages (Shona) as a medium of instruction in primary Schools. *Journal of Humanities and Social Science (IOSR-JHSS)*, 12(5), 58–65.

Chiwome, E. M. (1996). *A social history of the shona novel*. Eiffel Flats: Juta Zimbabwe Pty, Ltd.

Chumbow, B. S. (2009). Linguistic diversity, pluralism and national development in Africa. *Africa Development*, 34(2), 21–45.

Cohen, L., Manion, L., & Morrison, K. (2018). *Research methods in education* (10th ed.). London: Routledge.

Coleman, P., Collinge, J., & Seifert, T. (1983). Seeking the levers of change: Participant attitudes and school improvement. *School Effectiveness and School Improvement*, 4(1), 59–83.

Cooper, R.L. (1989). *Language planning and social change*. Cambridge: Cambridge University Press.

Creswell, J. W. (2014). *Research design: Qualitative, quantitative and mixed methods approaches* (4th ed.). London: Sage.

Doke, C. (1931). *Report on the unification of the Shona dialects*. Hertford: Austin.

Dube, M. (2012). The Zimbabwe indigenous languages promotion association (ZILPA) position paper, presented in the faculty of education, University of Zimbabwe. Retrieved September 12, 2012.

Gay, L. R., Mills, G. E., & Airasian, P. (2009). *Educational research competencies for analysis and application*. Columbus: Pearson.

Giliomee, H. (1997). Surrender without defeat: Afrikaners and the South African 'miracle'. *Daedalus*, 126(2), 113–146.

Goodman, S., & Graddol, D. (1996). *Resisting English: New texts, new identities*. London: Routledge.

Gora, R., Mavunga, G., Muringani, B., & Waniwa, F. (2010). The use of shona as a medium of instruction in the first three grades of primary school in Tonga speaking community: Parents' and teachers' perceptions. *Zimbabwe Journal Educational Research*, 22(1), 87–102.

Gora, R. B. (2014). Perception and attitude towards the study of African languages in Zimbabwean high schools: Implications for human resources development and management. Unpublished DPhil Thesis. Pretoria: University of South Africa.

Gora, R. B., & Mutasa, D. E. (2015). Impact of perception and attitude towards the study of African languages on human resource needs: A case of Zimbabwe. *Per Linguam, 31*(1), 74–88.

Government of Zimbabwe. (1987). *Zimbabwe education act.* Harare: Government Printers.

Gudhlanga, E. S. (2005). Promoting the use and teaching of African languages in Zimbabwe. *The Zimbabwe Journal of Educational Research, 17*(1), 54–68.

Gumbi P., & Ndimande-Hlongwa, N. (2015). Embracing the use of African languages as additional languages of T & L in KwaZulu-Natal Schools. *South African Journal of African Languages, 35*(2), 157–162.

Hachipola, S. J. (1998). *A survey of the minority languages of Zimbabwe.* Harare: University of Zimbabwe Publications.

Hapanyengwi-Chemhuru, O., & Makuvaza, N. (2014). Hunhu: In search of an indigenous philosophy for the Zimbabwean education system: Practice without thought is blind: Thought without practice is empty. *Journal of Indigenous Social Development, 3*(1), 1–15.

Hatori, R. (2005). A policy of language education in Japan: Beyond nationalism and linguicism. *Second Language Studies, 23*(2), 45–69.

Heldring, L., & Robinson, J. A. (2012). Colonialism and development in Africa. National Bureau of Economic Research Working Paper, 18566.

Henriksen, S. (2010). Language attitudes in a primary school: A bottom-up approach to language education policy in Mozambique. Unpublished. DPhil Thesis, Roskild University, Department of Culture, and Identity.

Hitachi Systems & Service. (2003). *My pedia.* Tokyo: Heibonsha.

Howie, S., Combrinck, C. M., Roux, K., & Palane, M. (2017). *Progress in international reading literacy study (PIRLS) 2016: South African highlights report.* Pretoria: University of Pretoria.

Hult, F. M., & Pietikäinen, S. (2014). Shaping discourses of multilingualism through a language ideological debate: The case of Swedish in inland. *Journal of Language and Politics, 13,* 1–20.

Hungwe, K. (2007). Language policy in Zimbabwean education: Historical antecedents and contemporary issues. *Compare, 37*(2), 135–149.

Jansen, D., & Warren, K. (2020). What (exactly) is research methodology? A plain-language explanation and definition (with examples). Retrieved March 6, 2020, from https://ww.gradcoach.com.

Jones, S. (1985). Depth interviews. In R. Walker (Ed.), *Applied quantitative research* (pp. 45–55). New York: Gower.

Kaarsholm, P. (1987). Interview with E Walter Krog, Harare.

Kaarsholm, P. (n.d.). The past as battlefield in Rhodesia and Zimbabwe: The struggle of competing nationalisms over history from colonisation to independence. Harare: Zimbabwe Printers.

Kahari, G. P. (1986). *Aspects of the Shona novel: And other related genres.* Gweru: Mambo Press.

Kamwangamalu, N. M. (2001). The language planning situation in South Africa. *Current Issues in Language Planning, 2*(4), 361–445.

Kamwendo, G. (1999). The political dimension of mother tongue instruction in Malawi. In L. Limage (Ed.) *Comparative perspectives on language and literacy.* Dakar: UNESCO, 232–243.

Kaplan, R. B., & Baldauf, R. B. (1997). *Language planning from practice to theory.* Clevedon: Multilingual Matters.

Kariati, M. (2001). Zimbabwe clubs ordered to play behind closed doors, AllAfrica, 31 January 2001. Retrieved January 24, 2023, from https://allafrica.com/stories/200101310287.html.

Kaschula, R. H., & Wolf, H. E. (2016). *Challenges: Linguistic plurality and diversity - Problem or resource?* Cambridge: Cambridge University Press.

Kayambazinthu, E. (2000). The language-planning situation in Malawi. *Journal of Multilingual and Multicultural Development, 19*(5&6), 369–439.

Kishindo, P. J. (2000). Language and development. *The Lamb, 2*(25), 14–15.

Koster, J. D. (1996). Managing the transformation. In K. Bekker (Ed.), *Citizen participation in local government* (pp. 99–118). Pretoria: Van Schaik.

Kuyedzwa, C. (2020). Zimbabwe VP blames colonisers for not teaching locals how to run economy. *Fin24*, 05 July 2020. Retrieved May 11, 2022, from https://www.news24.com.

Lee, R. M. (1993). *Doing research on sensitive topics.* London: Sage Publications.

Lin, J. (1997). Policies and practices of bilingual education for the minorities in China. *Journal of Multilingual and Multicultural Development, 18*(3), 193–205.

Lindlof, T., & Taylor, B. (2002). *Qualitative communication research methods.* London: Sage.

Mabvurira, V. (2020). Hunhu/ubuntu philosophy as a guide for ethical decision making in social work. *African Journal of Social Work, 10*(1), 73–81.

Mackey, W. F. (1979). Language policy and language planning. *Journal of Communication, 29*(2), 48–53.

Magwa, W. (2003). Planning for the future: Exploring possibilities of using indigenous African languages as languages of instruction in education: The Zimbabwean experience. Unpublished DPhil thesis. University of South Africa, Pretoria.

Magwa, W. (2015). Attitudes towards the use of indigenous African languages as languages of instruction in education: A case of Zimbabwe. *IISTE, 2*(1), 1–16.

Maja, I. (2007). Towards the protection of minority languages in Africa. Unpublished PhD Thesis. University of Ghana.

Mangaliso, M. P. (2001). Building competitive advantage from ubuntu: Management lessons from South Africa. *Academy of Management Perspectives, 15*(3), https://doi.org/10.5465/ame.2001.5229453.

Mazrui, A. (2002). The Asmara declaration on African languages: A critical reappraisal. A keynote address delivered at the annual conference of linguistics held at Ohio University, Athens, Ohio.

Mazrui, A. A., & Mazrui, A. M. (1997). *The power of babel: Language and governance in the African experience.* Chicago, IL: University of Chicago Press.

Mazrui, A. M. (1981). *Acceptability in a planned standard: The case of Swahili in Kenya.* Stanford: ProQuest Publishing.

Mazrui, A. A. (1993). Language and the quest for liberation in Africa: The legacy of Frantz Fanon. *Third World Quarterly, 14*(2), 351–363.

Mazrui, A. A. (2001). *Out of the count: The 1997 general elections and prospects for democracy in Kenya.* Kampala: Fountain Publishers.

Mbigi, L., & Maree, J. (1997). *Ubuntu: The spirit of African transformation management.* Johannesburg: Knowledge Resources.

Mchazime, H. S. (1999). Mother-tongue education in Malawi: Some implication for planning implementation and monitoring. In G. H. Kamwendo (Ed.), *Towards a national language policy in education proceedings of a national symposium on language policy formulation.*

Mhute, I. (2021). Language and communication in the education of Africa. In G. Motsaathebe (Ed.), *Education in Africa: Perspectives, opportunities and challenges* (pp. 31–46). New York: NOVA Science Publishers.

Mhute, I., Jakaza, E., & Mangeya, H. (2021). 'One of the finest English speakers Zimbabwe has ever had': Impact of Robert Gabriel Mugabe's exoglossic language policy on the development of Zimbabwe. In C. Sabao, R. R. Mahomva, & L. Mhandara (Eds.), *Re/membering Robert Gabriel Mugabe: Politics, legacy, philosophy, life and death*. Bulawayo: Leaders for Africa Network Readers.

Mhute, I., Mangeya, H., & Jakaza, E. (2022). *Endangering the endangered: A case of fake COVID-19 social media news in Zimbabwe*. Willington, DE: Generis Publishers.

Mhute, I., & Musingafi, M. C. C. (2014). The language question, development and the education of the disadvantaged through open and distance learning (ODL): A case of the Zimbabwe Open University (ZOU). *Asian Journal of Social Sciences and Management Studies*, *1*(2), 40–47.

Mhute, I., & Musingafi, M. C. C. (2015). Centrality of language in development: A case of Zimbabwe. *Journal of Economics and Sustainable Development*, *6*(20), 181–190.

Micheletti, G. (2010). Re-envisioning Paulo Freire's banking concept of education. *Inquiries Journal*, *2*(2), 312–320.

Mike, L. (1997). The language of reproduction: Is it doctored? *Qualitative Health Research*, *7*(2), 7–22. https://doi.org/10.1177/104973239700700202.

Ministry of Primary and Secondary Education (MoPSE) (2015). *Curriculum framework for primary and secondary education 2015–2022*. Harare: Government Printers.

Mkanganwi, K. G. (1992). Language planning in Southern Africa. In N. T. Crawhall (Ed.), *Democratically speaking: International perspectives on language planning* (pp. 6–11). South Africa. Harare: National Language Project.

Mkuti, L. D. (1996). *Language and education in Mozambique since 1940: Policy, implementation, and future perspectives*. New York: UMI.

Moloketi, G. R. (2009). Towards a common understanding of corruption in Africa. *Public Policy and Admiration*, *24*(3), 331–338. https://doi.org/10.1177/0952076709103814.

Moto, F. (2002). African language and the crisis of identity: The case of Malawi. In F. R. Owino (Ed.), *Speaking African languages for education and development* (pp. 33–44). Cape Town: CASAS.

Moyana, H., & Sibanda, M. (1984). *The African heritage: History for junior secondary schools: Book 4*. Harare: Zimbabwe Publishing House.

Moyo, T. (2002). Language politics and national identity in Malawi. *Southern African Journal of African Languages*, *4*, 262–272.

Msindo, E. (2005). Language and ethnicity in Matabeleland: Ndebele-Kalanga relations in Southern Zimbabwe, 1930–1960. *The International Journal of Historical Studies*, *38*(1), 79–103.

Mugumbate, J., & Nyanguru, A. (2013). Exploring African philosophy: The value of ubuntu in social work. *African Journal of Social Work*, *3*(1), 82–100.

Mutasa, D. E. (2003). The language policy of South Africa: What do people say? Unpublished DPhil Thesis. University of South Africa, Pretoria.

References

Mutasa, D. E. (2004). *People speak: Language policy and language in South Africa*. Pretoria: S.G. Publishers.

Ndlovu-Gatsheni, S. J. (2015). *Decolonisation, development and knowledge in Africa: Turning over a new leaf*. New York and London: Routledge.

Ndlovu-Gatsheni, S. J. (2020). *Decolonization, knowledge and development in Africa: Turning over a new leaf*. New York: Routledge.

Ndlovu, E., & Du Plessis, T. (2018). *Language as a means of achieving quality education and other sustainable development goals in Africa*. Harare: Human Resources Centre.

Ngara, E. A. (1982). *Bilingualism, language contact and language planning: Proposal for language use and language teaching in Zimbabwe*. Gweru: Mambo Press.

Nhongo, R. (2013). A national language policy for Zimbabwe in the twenty-first century: Myth or reality? *Journal of Language Teaching and Research*, 4(6), 1208–1215.

Noyes, A. R. (2020). *A new Zimbabwe: Assessing continuity and change after Mugabe*. Santa Monica, CA: RAND Corporation.

Nussbaum, B. (2003). Ubuntu: Reflections of a South African on our common humanity. *Reflections*, 4, 21–26. https://doi:1162/152417303322004175.

Nyaungwa, O. (2013). Exploring the feasibility of using shona as a medium of instruction in teaching science in Zimbabwe. Unpublished DPhil Thesis, UNISA.

Ocheni, S., & Nwankwo, B. S. (2012). Analysis of colonialism and its impact in Africa. *Cross-Cultural Communication*, 8(3), 46–54.

Official Government of Zimbabwe Web Portal. History of Zimbabwe colonisation. www.zim.gov.zw.

Oliver, E., & Oliver, W. H. (2017). The colonisation of South Africa: A unique case. *HTS Theological Studies*, 73(3), 232–241.

Ouane, A., & Glanz, C. (2011). Optimising learning, education and publishing in Africa: The language factor - A review and analysis of theory and practice in mother-tongue and bilingual education in sub-saharan Africa. UNESCO Institute for Lifelong Learning, Hamburg, Germany.

Penny, W. K. (2002). Linguistic imperialism: The role of English as an International Language. MA TEFL/TESL University of Birmingham.

Pennycook, A. (2001). *A critical applied linguistics: A critical introduction* (1st ed.). Routledge.

Pennycook, A. (2006). Language policy and the ecological turn. *Language Policy*, 3, 213–239.

Phillipson, R. (1992). *Linguistic Imperialism*. Oxford: Oxford University.

Pindula news 9 November 2022.

Prah, K. K. (2002). Language of instruction for education development and African emancipation. In B. Brock-Utne & R. K. Thompson (Eds.), *Languages of instruction for African emancipation: Focus on post-colonial contexts and considerations* (pp. 23–50). Cape Town: The Centre for Advanced Studies of African Society.

Prinsloo, E. D. (2000). Ubuntu culture and participatory management. In P. H. Coetzee & A. P. J. Roux (Eds.), *The African philosophy reader*. New York: Routledge.

Raftopolous, B. (2009). An overview of the GPA: National conflict regional agony and international dilemma. In B. Raftopolous (Ed.), *The hard reform: The politics of Zimbabwe's global political agreement*. Harare: Weaver Press.

Ranger, T. O. (1985). *The invention of tribalism in Zimbabwe*. Gweru: Mambo Press.

Ranger, T. O. (1989). Missionaries, migrants and the Manyika: The invention of ethnicity in Zimbabwe. In L. Vail (Ed.), *The creation of tribalism in Southern Africa*. London: James Currey.

Ranger, T. O. (2001). Democracy and traditional political structures in Zimbabwe, 1890–1999. In N. Bhebhe & T. O. Ranger (Eds.), *The historical dimensions of democracy and human rights in Zimbabwe* (pp. 31–52). Harare: University of Zimbabwe Publications.

Rasmussen, D. (1979). Praxis and social theory. *Human Studies*, *4*(1), 273–278.

Rhodesia Literature Bureau. (1979). *Gwenyambira*. Gweru: Mambo Press.

Ricento, T. (2000). Historical and theoretical perspectives in language policy and planning. In T. Ricento (Ed.), *Ideology, politics and language policies: Focus on English*. New York: John Benjamins.

Ricento, T. (Ed.). (2006). *Introduction to language policy: Theory and method*. London: Blackwell Publishers.

Roy-Campbell, Z. M., & Gwete, W. B. (1997). *Language and policy planning*. Harare: Zimbabwe Open University.

Samkange, S. J. W.T., & Samkange, S. (1980). *Hunhuism or ubuntuism: A Zimbabwe indigenous political philosophy*. Harare: Graham Publishing.

Schiffman, H. (2006). *Language policy and linguistic culture*. London: Blackwell Publishers.

Shizha, E., & Kariwo, M. (2011). *Education and development in Zimbabwe: A social, political and economic analysis*. New York: Rotterdam.

Shizha, E. (2012). Reclaiming and re-visioning indigenous voices: The case of the language of instruction in science education in Zimbabwean primary schools'. *Literacy Information and Computer Education Journal (LICEJ), Special Issue*, *1*(1), 785–793.

Sibanda, L. (2019). Zimbabwe language policy: Continuity or radical change? *Journal of Contemporary Issues in Education*, *14*(2), 2–15.

Skutnabb-Kangas, T. (1988). Multilingualism and the education of minority children. In T. Skutnabb-Kangas & J. Cummins (Eds.), *Minority education: From shame to struggle* (pp. 9–44). Clevedon: Multilingual Matters.

Skutnabb-Kangas, T., & Phillipson, R. (Eds.). (1994). *Linguistic human rights: Overcoming linguistic discrimination*. Berlin: Mouton de Gruyter.

South Africa. (1996). *The South African schools act (Act number 84)*. Pretoria: Government Printers.

Spolsky, B. (2009). *Language management*. Cambridge: Cambridge University Press.

Statistics South Africa. (2012). *Census 2011 census in brief*. Pretoria: Statistics South Africa. Retrieved November 13, 2022, from http://www.statssa.gov.za/census2011/Products/Census_2011_Census_in_brief.pdf.

Tackie-Ofosu, V., Mahama, S., Dosoo, V. E. ST, Kumador, D. K., & Toku, N. A. A. (2015). Mother tongue usage in Ghanaian pre-schools: Perceptions of parents and teachers. *Journal of Education and Practice*, *6*(34), 81–87.

Teasley, C., & Butler, A. (2020). Intersecting critical pedagogies to counter coloniality. In *The SAGE handbook of critical pedagogies* (Vol. 3, pp. 277–289).

The Catholic Commission for Justice and Peace in Zimbabwe and The Legal Resources Foundation. (1997). *Breaking the silence, building true peace: A report on the disturbances in Matabeleland and the Midlands 1980 to 1988*. Harare: Africa Synod House.

The News Day Weekender 9 November 2022.

The Patriot August 31, 2017.

The World Bank. https://documents.worldbank.org.

Tsodzo, T. K. (1982). *Tsodzo*. Gweru: Mambo Press.

Tutu, D. (2004). *God has a dream: A vision of hope for our time*. London: Rider.

UJU, C. C. (2008). Language, science, technology and mathematics and poverty alleviation in Africa: A case of Nigeria. *Zimbabwe Journal of Educational Research*, *20*(1), 22–29.

Umeogu, B., & Ifeoma, O. (2012). Cultural dependency: A philosophical insight. *Open Journal of Philosophy*, *2*(2), 123–127.

UNESCO. (1953). *The use of vernacular language in education*. Paris: UNESCO.

Watts, M., & Ebbutt, D. (1987). More than the sum of the parts: Research methods in group interviewing. *British Educational Research Journal*, *13*(1), 25–34.

Wa Thiong'o, N. (1987). *Decolonising the mind: The politics of language in African literature*. London: James Currey.

Wolff, H. E. (2016). *Language and development in Africa*. Cambridge: Cambridge University Press.

Wolfgang, M. (1973). The language question in the colonial policy of German imperialism. *African Studies*, *1*(1), 383–397.

Woodberry, R. D. (2011). Ignoring the obvious: What explains Botswana's exceptional democratic and economic performance in sub-saharan Africa. Project on Religion and Economic Change Working Paper #05

Woolf, P. (1997). History and imperialism: A century of theory from Marx to post colonialism. *American Historical Review*, *1*(2), 133–144.

Zhou, M. (2000). Language policy and illiteracy in ethnic minority communities in China. *Journal of Multilingual and Multicultural Development*, *21*(2), 129–148.

Zimbabwe Observer 12 March 2022. https://zimbabweobserver.com.au/2022/03/12/.

Index

2013 declaration on language use 45

African traditional religion 58
assimilation 16

'centre' 6, 48
Chilapalapa 27
chiraparapa 27
colonial administrations 1
colonial agenda 13
colonial clutch 3
colonial educational reform 68
colonial hegemony 70
Colonialism 1, 5, 17, 53
colonialist-inspired migration 59
coloniality 1
colonial language policy 47, 73, 79, 82
colonial machine x
colonial parameters 6
coloniser's mandate 1
complete assimilation 5
complete transformations 6
'complex language' 68
compulsory language 42
Core 6
critical applied linguistics 7
Critical Language Policy (CLP) theory 7, 12, 17, 25, 39, 67
cultural dependency 57
cultural diversity 57
cultural suppression 19
Culturecide 53

decolonising education 78
developing post-colonies 7
divide-and-rule ideology 36

eating habits 60
economic development 42
economic exploitation 2
economic imperialism 2, 5, 18–20, 24, 40
economic implications 39
educational imperialism 5, 21, 70
educational language policy 71, 72
elimination of epistemology 56
emancipatory effort 2
English lifestyle 65
enlightenment 1
ethnocide 53
Eurocentric hegemonic power relationships 78
evolutionist perception 68
expansionist politics 16
exploitation 1, 2, 19, 41

feeding relationship 2
formal Imperialism 5, 6
forms of imperialism 2–3

global inequalities 6
Gukurahundi 31, 36, 62

hegemonic societal dominance 41
Hunhu/Unhu/Ubuntu 61, 62, 63, 65, 84, 87

illegal sanctions 3
Individualism 61, 65
Imperialism 5
indigenous culture 58
indigenous identity 53
Indigenous knowledge systems 20, 21, 48

Index

indigenous languages 5, 24, 42, 45, 47, 51, 53, 56–57, 69, 81
Individualism 61, 65
informal versus 5, 6
intangible heritage 20, 21, 59
Intergovernmental Conference on Language Policies in Africa (ICLPA) 20
Internationalisation 15
irredeemably primitive 53

language attitude 15
language engineering 13
Language ideology 14–15
language management 13
language of administration 36
language of imperialism 68
language of instruction 42, 69
language planning 13–14, 79
language policy 2, 7, 17–18, 20, 35, 66, 75, 79
liberation movement 2
linguicism 4, 20
linguistic Africanisation 4
linguistic agenda 4
linguistically inspired dependency syndrome 50
linguistic assimilation 15
linguistic community 14
linguistic configuration 35
linguistic democracy 74
linguistic emancipation 46
linguistic hierarchisation 4
linguistic ideology 14, 16
linguistic imperialism 1–8, 10–17, 18, 20–22, 24–25, 36–37, 39, 41, 46–47, 50, 57–60, 62, 64–65, 75, 79, 80–81, 84–86
Linguistic pluralism 15
linguistic terrorism 53
local traditional religion 52
look east policy' mantra 3
look west policy 3

marginalisation of local languages 16
marginalised language speakers 35
medieval states 1

minoritised languages 77
modern territories 1
multiplicity of languages 13
mutually interlocking types of imperialism 16

national administrations 6
national and minority language cultures 59

'periphery' 6
pidgin language 17, 27
political domination 2
political emancipation/ independence 25, 46, 56
political ideology 18
political imperialism 2, 5, 24, 29, 40, 46, 86
post-colonial language policy 54
pre-colonial hatred 29
pre-existing knowledges 53
prestigious language 41
priceless knowledge 59

real emancipation 2, 12
regime change agenda 3
Regionalism 31

sociocultural hierarchy 2
sociocultural imperialism 2, 5, 20, 24, 63
sociocultural transformation 65
Southern Rhodesian language policy 7, 59
Southern Rhodesian linguistic agenda 12, 18, 25, 57, 76
The Southern Rhodesian linguistic configuration 43
Southern Rhodesian linguistic imperialism 11, 67
structures of dependency 6
subtractive bilingualism 72

traditional education 70
traditional herbs 48
traditional knowledge systems 46, 48, 59
tricky treaties 6

unfair diglossic landscape 75
Universal Declaration on Linguistic
  Rights 56
utility beauty 64

Vernacularisation 15

Zimbabwean languages and
  cultures 48
zones of sovereignty and
  privileges 6